"You blessed me big time with this book, and I pray that God will use this to encourage all who are in the cities throughout the U.S. . . . . Thank you so very much for reminding me of God's goodness and mercy in the little things amidst the chaos!"

—Brian Bakke
Director of Community Ministries
and New Flight Art Ministry at
Uptown Baptist Church, Chicago

"The struggles of an urban missionary were never more clearly described than Field's *A Church Called Graffiti*. I commend it to anyone who wants to be challenged by sacrificial ministry."

—David R. Dean
Executive Director,
Metropolitan New York Baptist Association

"How often do I catch myself praying for God to be part of my agenda rather than the other way around? Nothing sets me straight again like the time I spend with the folks at Graffiti, and no book you read this year will inspire you more with the desire to be on the same page with what God is doing in our world today. This is the real deal."

—Kyle Matthews
Christian Singer/Songwriter,
Nashville

"In our day we too often see people who 'talk the talk' but don't 'walk the walk.' When it comes to effective ministry that impacts the city, Taylor Field has the walk that backs up the talk. He has invested his life, and his family's, in one of the world's most challenging arenas—New York City. And he's making a lasting impact. Walk with him through the Big Apple and watch Jesus touch lives today . . . just as he did in Jericho, Jerusalem, and the cities of his day. You'll see our cities from a whole new view—through the eyes of Jesus."

—Dr. Bob Reccord
President, North American Mission Board, SBC

"Long before you have finished reading *A Church Called Graffiti,* one of the words that will cross your mind repeatedly is *gratitude.* . . . You will be moved to tears by the generosity of so many who had so little, in sharing and encouraging others as they struggle for survival."

—Zig Ziglar
Author, Motivational Teacher

a Church Called Graffiti

(finding grace
on the
Lower East Side

a Church
Called
Graffiti

Taylor Field

with Jo Kadlecek

BROADMAN
& HOLMAN
PUBLISHERS

nashville, tn

0-8054-2369-9

Published by Broadman & Holman Publishers,
Nashville, Tennessee

Dewey Decimal Classification: 277
Subject Heading: CHURCH MINISTRY
Library of Congress Card Catalog Number: 2001035485

Photos courtesy of the North American Mission Board of the Southern Baptist Convention and author Taylor Field.

Unless otherwise stated, all Scripture citation is from the Holy Bible, New International Version, © 1973, 1978, 1984 by International Bible Society. The other translation cited is NRSV, New Revised Standard Version of the Bible, © 1989 by the Division of Christian Education of the National Council of Churches of Christ in the United States of America, used by permission, all rights reserved.

Library of Congress Cataloging-in-Publication Data
Field, Taylor.
    A church called Graffiti : finding grace on the
    Lower East Side / Taylor Field with Jo Kadlecek.
        p. cm.
    Includes bibliographical references.
    ISBN 0-8054-2369-9
    1. Church work. 2. East Seventh Baptist Church (New York,
N.Y.). 3. City churches. I. Kadlecek, Jo. II. Title.

BV4447 .F544   2001
277.47'10829—dc21
                                                        2001035485
                                                        CIP
        1 2 3 4 5 6 7 8 9 10 05 04 03 02 01

To Susan, my soul mate.

Contents

Foreword

Long before you have finished reading *A Church Called Graffiti*, one of the words that will cross your mind repeatedly is *gratitude*. That's what you will feel for the work and ministry that Taylor Field has been called to do, and you will probably be grateful that God did not call you to a similar ministry.

You will read some amazing things about people, many of whom never had a chance. Men and women who are "strange" because they are "different." You'll meet a woman who had an addiction to collecting trash, thought it was all she had, and so completely filled her home with it there was room for nothing else, including bathroom facilities. You'll meet a drug dealer who had a huge influence on the neighborhood and felt that he was an asset though he was guilty of getting many of them hooked on cocaine. True, he "protected" his block, but when he was put in prison the neighborhood improved and he met Christ. His faith is strong, and he is excited about what Christ has done for him.

You will walk with Taylor Field as he journeys into the unknown, meeting people in frightening circumstances, learning to love and encourage them. Along the way he was accepted and through God's grace brought them hope. You will see him fight for the homeless, encourage the discouraged, defend the defenseless, and, through it all, learn some valuable lessons from people most of us would consider out of reach.

You will meet, misunderstand, and come to know Sam, whose constant companion was a butcher knife, and you will watch him grow but never quite make it. Yet, he had an impact on those around him and, in the process, even taught Dr. Field some lessons. You will come to know the hopeless people who gradually developed trust and found hope in this commitment that drives Taylor Field to serve in this unique ministry.

You'll watch as he meets alcoholics, dope addicts, petty thieves, prostitutes, the illiterate, and people for whom it would take the love of Christ to impact their lives. Yet, Taylor Field has managed to minister to these people, come to love them, and find his home in their community. You will feel the heat and humidity and smell the sweat of the community where the church is the only lighthouse for the hopeless.

You will sense Taylor's fear in the early days of his ministry when he imagined all sorts of things happening to his wife, Susan, when she was late returning home one day. Your imagination will take you into the pitch dark deserted building with the missing stairs and marvel that some unknown face in the building helped Taylor climb the steps, looking for a fourteen-year-old who had run away from home.

You'll be amazed by the Bible study with alcoholics and those who were slightly deranged. You will be amazed and rejoice at the little victories that ultimately led to a different community, a different environment, and a different outlook on life that includes hope. You will be amazed at how an educated middle class theologian, who had lived an entirely different lifestyle, could ever experience joy in serving people who were so different from anything he had ever known. Eventually, you will begin to understand the joy in his heart, as through Christ he was able to effect some significant changes.

You will be moved to tears by the generosity of so many who had so little in sharing and encouraging others as they struggled for survival. Before you finish *A Church Called Graffiti*, you will do a little weeping with joy that regardless of how hopeless the situation looks, you will become convinced that, with God's help, it can be changed. Your own commitment, as a result, will be stronger and your effectiveness will increase. You will even catch yourself saying from time to time, "Hot dog! This is it!"

—Zig Ziglar, author/motivational teacher
Carrollton, Texas

Thank you. That is my philosophy.
Thank you very much.
—A CONTEMPORARY ARTIST

Acknowledgments

I give many thanks to the people in our neighborhood who showed so much courage in such tough situations. Names, details, and time sequences have sometimes been changed to protect people's confidentiality or to clarify the story.

Many thanks to countless coworkers in our ministry and work teams. Some have worked for years and years; others, for short periods. Their combined work in the name of Christ has changed our neighborhood. There are a number of stories of God's grace that I did not include.

Many thanks to the churches in our city and in the nation who reached out to our neighborhood. For them, the terms *hunger, homelessness,* and *drug abuse* did not relate to issues, but to people.

Many thanks to those who helped us launch this book. Zig Ziglar became an encourager and helped us make contact with his agent, Bruce Barbour, who in turn helped us contact Broadman & Holman.

Many thanks to Jo Kadlecek, who worked tirelessly to put the stories I wrote together. Her patience and thoughtfulness are greatly appreciated.

Many thanks to Susan, my wife, who helped write, edit, review, revise, and remember the many adventures we have gone through together.

Finally, many thanks to God, who has shown me so clearly how precious he holds us, even when he, and we, have been scarred.

Dirt glitters when the
sun happens to shine.
—GOETHE

chapter one
Different Planets

The blade of a butcher knife was sticking out through the bottom of Sam's plastic grocery bag when he intercepted me on the street one day. I often met Sam on the street, and I usually stopped to listen to his jokes and talk about everything imaginable. He had been attending our Bible studies on the Lower East Side; and though I knew this short, thin man with a shaggy head of hair had a great sense of humor, I also knew he was easily angered. This day, Sam couldn't seem to stop talking, but the sharp end of the knife, jutting out like the head of a shark, had my full attention.

"Sam, what's that in your bag?" I asked quietly.

"Oh, that's a butcher knife," he said.

"Well, what are you going to do with it?"

Sam narrowed his eyes and looked into the distance. He spoke with conviction. "I'm going over to Joe's house to cut his

1

eye out with it." Joe—a Vietnam veteran who wore army fatigues, a knife strapped to his leg, and a Palestinian scarf—had also been at the same little Bible study where Sam and I had been the night before.

"Well, why are you going to cut him up?"

"Because I gave him fifty dollars to buy me some dope yesterday, and he didn't do it. He doesn't know me. I'm crazy. I'm a nut-job! I'll cut him up!" Sam looked up at the sky and down at the street. His shoulders were shaking as he sucked in air. Foam began to collect at the corners of his mouth.

"No . . . no," I stuttered. I'd only been at Graffiti Ministries a few weeks. "Don't do that! Don't you remember the song we sang last night: 'They'll Know We Are Christians by Our Love'?" I tried to hum a few bars to remind him. Sam looked at the sidewalk with his mouth wide open, shaking his head. "Come on now, Sam," I continued, "let's *talk* it out; don't act it out. Let's go to Joe and see if we can talk this through." Reluctantly, he followed me to Joe's.

Joe lived in a tenement building two blocks away. His door was at the end of a dreary hall, and the whole place smelled like a catbox. Most of the linoleum had been stripped off the floor, and paint was dangling from the walls in long gray streaks. When I finally found Joe's apartment, there must have been six locks on the door. I didn't exactly feel welcomed, but I knocked anyway. "Who?" Joe shouted.

As Sam paced the hall behind me, I explained to Joe why we were there. It was soon clear that Joe was not going to open that door for anything. I used all the powers of reasoning I could think of to get the two men to work things out. "Come on, open the door, Joe," I shouted at the locks. "Let's talk this out!" Nothing happened. I kept shouting. The catbox odor got worse.

Sam paced; Joe shouted back. Fifteen minutes passed, and as we stood outside the door in that dingy hallway, I became more and more anxious about working things out. Then, all of a sudden, I realized what was happening.

Wait a minute; what am I doing? I thought. *Here I am a pastor-missionary, first month on the job in New York City, dewy-eyed, wet behind the ears, and I am standing here in a hallway negotiating a drug deal!*

Maybe Sam sensed what I was thinking because within seconds he ran out of the building with his knife, disgruntled and distracted. He stalked off across the park, holding his knife in his grocery bag. I went back to the mission storefront, dazed, and sighed at the thought of seeing Joe next week with his eye removed. Thankfully, Sam apparently calmed down eventually because Joe came to Bible study with both eyes intact—the two men had worked it out without my help.

My encounter with Sam and his butcher knife was one of my first introductions to this city, a city where worlds collide so regularly that the collisions and their ensuing chaos have become almost normal to me. My experience with these parallel worlds began in 1986 when my family and I moved to the Lower East Side of New York City and I became the pastor/director of the East Seventh Baptist Ministry (known around here as "Graffiti"). Since then, I've observed a thousand different stories like Sam's walk beside me on the streets, stories I could never have expected to read in all my life, stories that have caused me to redefine words like *normal* and *church, family* and *home, conflict* and *help.*

You see, where I grew up—a small town called Enid, Oklahoma—life was slower and more predictable. The entire population of forty thousand was sprinkled across a dozen or so miles (you could only fill a few city blocks around Graffiti with the same number of people). I grew up with folks who planned for the future and worked hard to achieve it. Many families looked like mine: we spent Sundays in church, Wednesday nights in prayer services, and the rest of the week working hard on a regular schedule. The last thing I expected when I left Enid was that someday I would live in a parallel galaxy like the Lower East Side, meeting people like Sam and Joe.

But now I can't imagine living anywhere else.

Growing up, though, I would never have imagined a church could be made of people who smelled so differently. Where I came from, church buildings were clean, people had nice teeth, and no one was outwardly violent. They always had a place to stay and rarely said what they really thought. They protected their spirits and their lives.

Here on the Lower East Side, however, I talk with people who don't know if they're going to eat tomorrow. Some who live in buildings that don't have heat get frostbite and sometimes have to have their toes amputated. I had never experienced the death of someone close to me until I came to New York. In the first year alone, one friend's throat was cut, another was burned to death in an abandoned building, another was so drunk he lay on a heater and died of burns to the bone, and another froze to death.

This was all new to me, a different planet altogether, a world that seminary did not necessarily prepare me for. Growing up in Oklahoma and then attending college in North Carolina, I had never been around people who were not competent, who could not find Genesis in their Bible, or, in fact, who could not read it at all. I had never known anyone before who was so furious when he didn't have the fifty dollars a friend owed him that he talked about stabbing the guy's eye out or bashing his head with a lead pipe. Yet, this same man goes out of his way to ask people what they need or tell them that they look great or laugh at any joke, funny or not. No one's ever cared about my birthday the way Sam did when he brought me five little presents he found on the street.

One friend lived in subway tunnels and had to compete with rats for food and shelter before he met Christ. Some of our neighbors are immigrants who have battled alcohol addiction all their lives, one of whom gave it up the day she asked a church member to pray with her so she could ask Christ into her life. Some of the people who come to our Bible study have lived on the street so long they wouldn't even stand near anyone or allow themselves to be touched at first. In fact, Sam threw garbage at a pastor until one day the pastor finally persuaded him to share a meal. It was still years before Sam trusted Christ as Lord.

In spite of all their pain, I have noticed that people here seem to laugh more. It is not the polite laughter one hears at some churches, where people are comfortable and secure but seem a little sad. No, here I think the people have more fun—they laugh with their mouth full and dance around the room where we have lunch or Bible studies. They tease more, hug more, get mad more, and they really do laugh more. I hear them.

If you walked into our church—Graffiti on East Seventh Street—as soon as you opened the door, you'd hear everyone shouting that they're glad you're here. In fact, everyone gets applause when they walk through the door, maybe even a hug. Sometimes it stinks like dirty socks, stale cigarettes, and old soup—especially because there are no windows and no ventilation. (Foot washing services here can be toxic.) You'd be greeted with Spanish and English jokes followed by belly laughs, loud and different and raucous. Some laugh for emphasis or just to show they're listening. Some cackle like chickens; others roar like bulls. Looking around, you'd see that some folks have come from the park where they sat outside all day, some have been on the "circuit" of social services where they get other free meals, while others have come from abandoned buildings or a friend's apartment or a long-term housing project. People wear layers of clothing in the winter, a few have hatchets or hammers in their belts, and many wear clothes they got from our clothes closet—hand-me-downs from some of our richer churches.

People here say what they're thinking too. I once overheard a conversation between two teenagers when one was inviting the other to our church, to which he replied, "No way. I'm not going there; it stinks." Another time, a man asked me, "If there's no such thing as luck, how come they make Lucky Charms?" And I can't forget when one friend proclaimed, "I don't mind when the Holy Spirit comes in. I just don't like it when he comes in sideways."

Here in our Lower East Side neighborhood, I think the Holy Spirit has indeed entered . . . sideways. To some it may seem a world of lunacy, a parallel galaxy, a place where any behavior seems to fit in. Perhaps it is most like an exhibit I recently saw at an art museum concerning the last fifty years of art. The paintings reflected minimalism, abstract expressionism, pop art, and a variety of other styles. Yet the exhibit focused on only one geographical area—the Lower East Side. They described how its "Bohemian Carnival-like atmosphere" in the late 1980s and early 1990s had a huge influence on the world of art and thought.

Similarly, when I think of our church here, I see a Bohemian Carnival-like atmosphere that is both disconcerting and wonderful. Disconcerting to me because I was not used to people who didn't know where they'd sleep each night or who speak their minds at the moment or who can be so generous that they'll give away the only slice of pizza they have. Wonderful because of their humor and the uniqueness of their perspectives (like the time Sam prayed, "God, since you're the Father and I'm your son, how about an allowance?"). On the Lower East Side, not everyone colors in the lines.

In my office at the church, I have a small photograph taken when the "carnival" first began for us. It is filled with faces of friends I will introduce in the following pages: immigrants, drug dealers, homeless men, frightened women, many of whom have died since we took that photo. Some of the folks in the photo have dealt with circumstances most of us could never imagine. For instance, there was the guy who always took care of his pit bull dog as if it were his only child. One day he watched, horrified, as a drug dealer took out his pistol and shot the dog right in front of him because he wouldn't sell it to him. The distraught man came to us and wept and grieved as one who had lost his child. He felt powerless. I can't help contrasting that to where I grew up, where power, supported by comfort, is taken for granted.

In the Book of Revelation, verse 21:8, there's a list of qualities of those who are going to hell, a list I call "the parade to hell." Those who chose personal safety and comfort over faithfulness to Christ lead the parade. At Graffiti, at our Bohemian Carnival, at our parallel planet, I see people who have not necessarily chosen comfort. I call them "monks in reverse"—they seem to have given up everything in pursuit of something they can't quite describe. Every other place I have been in my life has been one where comfort has been the goal. But here, people don't know—and sometimes don't care—what they're doing tomorrow.

From them, I have learned that weakness is the envelope for God's power. And that is what this book is about.

Welcome to the Lower East Side.
Now go home!
—GRAFFITI ON A WALL

chapter two
A Heart That Sings

LaGuardia Airport was hot, confusing, and unfriendly. I had not yet mastered the terminals and attitudes of New York's transportation whirlwind, so I was a bit nervous when I arrived. I had circled the parking lot so many times that I was afraid I was late. My wife, Susan, and our two infant sons were flying in from the midwest. They had spent a few weeks with our family while I found an apartment for us in the city. Their arrival, mixed with the hot June temperatures, made me anxious about what lay ahead.

Susan smiled as she got off the plane, and the kids squealed. My heart felt a little calmer. Still, I couldn't help wondering how she would feel climbing the creaking stairs and seeing the apartment I had finally secured: a tiny two-bedroom, fourth-floor walk-up on a noisy street on the Lower East Side. The walls were Pepto-Bismol pink, and since the electricity hadn't been turned on yet, we couldn't even use the fans. I had stayed there the night before, preparing and trying (in vain) to fall asleep in spite of the noises below—cars, unending police and ambulance sirens, trucks grinding, and people yelling into the morning hours. Boxes and suitcases were still strewn around the kitchen and hallway. It was not exactly the perfect home to which I wanted to bring my family. I was discouraged.

Still, Susan reminded me that we had "endured" awkward living conditions before, so she believed we could handle this too. In fact, I had met her in New York almost eight years before during a summer urban ministry program with the Baptist mission. She had been finishing college in Atlanta, and I was attending graduate school in New Jersey. Six months later we were engaged, and we both felt called to a life together in full-time ministry, wherever that might take us. In our first year of marriage we worked in Harlem on the weekends and during the summer while I finished seminary. The next two years of our marriage took us to Hong Kong, where I taught religion and philosophy at a Baptist college and Susan taught English.

By 1982 we were back in the United States where I pursued a Ph.D. in biblical studies. We lived two years on the seminary campus in San Francisco and one and a half in the city while I worked at a shelter for the homeless, still pursuing my degree. My father was not exactly happy that I was in school again, but I enjoyed studying, teaching, and writing my dissertation. Yet despite the studying and ministry opportunities in San Francisco, I began to experience a gnawing restlessness, the kind that made me wonder what specific direction I should be going to serve God. I felt like an armchair Christian, spending most of my time talking and theorizing about Christianity.

One day on campus, I sat in the chapel service and heard a speaker talk about the danger of comparing ourselves to others.

I stared at the floor, trying hard to make sense of what I was hearing. I thought of my family, of life in Oklahoma, New York, Hong Kong, and now California. The restlessness was rising. But then the speaker said something I have never forgotten, something that completely changed the course of my life, and my family's, and ultimately brought us back to New York's Lower East Side: "Find the one thing that you must do, and do it. How do you know what you must do? Here is a tip: Find the thing that makes your heart sing." I was riveted.

Sitting on that hard bench in the chapel, I realized what made my heart sing more than anything was not teaching, though I enjoyed it. Neither was it running an office or writing papers, though I didn't mind doing either. What really gave me an abiding joy was trying to express God's love in tangible ways to those who seemed to be hurting the most. The actual act of giving a sandwich, providing a blanket, or helping someone read gave me great joy. I knew at that moment where I wanted to be.

Susan agreed. We called Ray Gilliland, our Southern Baptist friend and mentor in New York. We had met Ray during our summer city program and appreciated his commitment to urban ministry. He was a crusty, one-eyed mentor whose raspy voice welcomed me on the telephone and then told me to "Come on out here!" when I explained what I'd like to do. The Southern Baptist Convention had planted Graffiti Ministries in 1974 as a mission to New York's Lower East Side. The mission had built a long tradition of Bible studies, meals to the homeless, and work with children. Ray told me that they wanted to plant a church to provide more stability for the ministries, and the pastor/director position was still open. I could apply for the job if I wanted it.

Susan and I made our decision, and I got the job. Once I finished seminary in the spring of 1986, I headed to New York to find an apartment while Susan and our boys visited with her family. I looked all over the neighborhood and around the church—from East Fourteenth Street to East First Street—for an apartment we could afford. It was not easy.

The Lower East Side was a study of contrasts, to be sure, and everywhere I went I ran into colliding worlds. Either landlords didn't show up for appointments, or the place was out of our price range. Housing rates had gone through the roof. In 1974, a two-bedroom apartment had been $65 a month. Now, twelve years later, the same apartment went for $1,200. Rent control motivated landlords to get folks out who were paying low rent. Graffiti on the walls said, "Death to Yuppies" and "The Park Belongs to the People." But once tenants lost their apartments, they usually couldn't afford another one. What's more, the presence of a strong drug culture, abandoned buildings, and runaways helped turn the area into a catchall for people falling through the cracks. City officials did not see affordable housing as a priority in this area, and they sometimes withheld funding for real estate development. Even though I knew this was the right place for my family, I also felt pushed around by the hustle and tensions of street life. I had no idea how God was going to provide for us.

Weeks before Susan's arrival with the boys, questions began to haunt me: Could we afford to buy? Should we live in a home in New Jersey, a home with a yard for the kids to grow up in? Should we commute into the city? Or was it better to actually have our home in the area where we'd be ministering? Though I was strongly in favor of the latter, I wondered if it was really possible. Could our "hearts sing" under these conditions?

Finally, I took the pink apartment next door to a crack house. The electricity had not been turned on yet, and the city was in the middle of a sweltering heat wave. We had no fan, no lights, no furniture, and no family close by. We only had a few new friends at our church. *This* was what I was bringing my wife and small sons home to from LaGuardia Airport. We even had to borrow old smelly cushions from another church to sleep on. I tried to be hopeful.

Thankfully, Susan looked at the pink walls, smiled, and took it all like a pioneer; she made the best of things. I stayed awake most of that first night, listening to constant sirens and the shouting in front of our apartment building, thinking, *I can't believe I just signed a year's lease to this place.* Many well-intentioned friends had advised me against moving into a place "like this," sometimes implying how foolish I was to bring my family here.

I was beginning to think they were right.

Cluttered Sidewalks

The next few weeks were filled with new sights and strange sounds for all of us. Susan and I tried to remember what it had been like when we had first moved to Hong Kong: smells we'd never known and words we'd never heard had swirled around us with the busy urban traffic. Now we were experiencing similar culture shock; I just didn't want to admit it. After all, this was the city where we'd fallen in love, the city where God had opened the door for us to pastor a little storefront ministry. We knew New York. What could be so hard?

The humidity was intense, and the scorching heat bounced off the pavement as I ran back and forth the seven blocks between our little apartment to check on Susan and the boys and the Graffiti building where I was leading Bible studies and summer programs. At the end of each hot day, I was exhausted.

Though we were still new to the ministry and neighborhood, I already felt the resources of my soul dwindling away. I often found myself praying that God would give me the gift of faith to see his design in the fabric of such frantic days. I felt overwhelming need everywhere I turned. My heart was no different.

To cool off from the sweatbox of our apartment one morning, we took the boys to the park. As we walked down the steps, my mind wandered to the first time I had visited this neighborhood. It was the summer before I met Susan, and I was struck then by the rows and rows of men lying on the hot sidewalk by Tompkins Square Park, many of them drunk or high or lost in their own painful world. Most of them were asleep; some were asking for money; many were just lonely. I remembered one older man in particular had somehow fallen into such a deep sleep that he didn't even realize his pants were down, excrement covering his clothes. Flies buzzed around him. As I passed the fires burning in the trash cans nearby, I thought I was walking through Dante's inferno.

The images from that time never seemed to fade. I had heard others call the park Dog Doo Park, for obvious reasons, so I always watched where I stepped. Puerto Rican and Hispanic older men played radios with Salsa music, drank Colt 45 beer at any time of day, and talked and argued in Spanish around park benches or cars. Scuffles and fights were as frequent as the blaring radios. In another part of the park—Dog Doo Hill—young Latino girls and boys played king of the hill. Teenage boys rode by on bicycles trying to impress their girlfriends. Streetlights were broken, and benches were destroyed. Beer and wine bottles in paper bags and moldy fruit were scattered across grass patches and sidewalks alike. With each step I took, the smell of urine smacked me in the face. Shouts of "Yo, white boy. Whatcha doing here?" hit my ears like fists. I remembered how quickly I had hurried from church toward the subway to get safely out of that apparent carnival of hell. If someone in those days had told me I would someday bring my wife and kids to live right around the corner, I would have said they were crazy. The images from that time never left my head.

Still, it had been almost ten years since my first visit here, and Tompkins Square Park was changing. Surely God would not have brought us to the same "carnival" I had seen years before, would he? Besides, I couldn't forget how often some of the people had surprised me with both their amazing circumstances and their unexpected generosity. Like the time when I was walking toward the park and a guy asked me to buy him a piece of pizza. When we left the restaurant, he asked me to wait a minute so he could go and give half to a friend. I was stunned.

No, Tompkins Square Park in 1986 is different, I told myself as I walked outside with our sons and toward the park that summer morning. I tried not to notice how the entry to the abandoned building next door was boarded with plywood to keep people out (although it hadn't accomplished its purpose). I pretended the twenty or so crack-cocaine vials that littered the sidewalk weren't really there. But when a grizzled man suddenly pushed open the plywood like a door and came out into the daylight, staring at us with a territorial glare, no amount of pretending could deny what was going on around us.

"Let's go to the park," I announced as we walked toward the spot with benches and trees a few blocks away. We strolled in the hot summer sun toward the park and even felt a slight breeze. Susan sat on a bench with the baby while I took two-year-old Freeman to a patch of grass and bushes. He was delighted to have free rein to run, and his little legs churned across the cobblestones and onto the grass.

"Oh, hurry, Freeman, come here. Look at this squirrel!" I shouted as we got close to the trees. He hurried to catch a glimpse of the little furry creature, but the closer we got, the more I realized my mistake. After a few steps, my heart sank. The animal skittering across the bottom of the tree wasn't a squirrel at all; it was a long fat rat, turning its proud ugly head toward the sidewalk and strutting its way toward my son. Even the rat had an attitude.

"Oh, let's go look at some other things," I told Freeman, grabbing his hand and hurrying away. A deep sigh of disappointment rose from my lungs.

We walked back to our apartment, and from our window we could see people selling drugs openly on the street, children playing around crack vials, and men going in and out of abandoned buildings. The despair was so visible, so real to me, and though Susan was upbeat and optimistic about it all, I was fearful. What had I done?

One Wednesday night I was at Graffiti's center, and Susan and the kids were supposed to walk the seven blocks over and walk home with me after church. I finished our Bible study and looked at my watch—Susan and our sons were not there. It was getting late, and I began to worry. I had passed men staggering down the streets, the trash cans on fire. More and more homeless men were coming outside of their squatter buildings to catch a summer breeze, and it seemed like every corner I turned down was a drug supermarket. Was I risking my family's well-being by being here? They had to walk through the same park that had smelled of feces and urine. Only now it was dubbed Tent City. Was this the right thing? Where were they?

By the time I was sweeping up and locking the doors, I was tense. Still no sign of Susan and the boys. The heat was miserable. The people were needy. What was God trying to teach me?

I hurried past the people living in cardboard boxes or makeshift tents put together with blankets or garbage bags. Rags, ropes, plastic, and a few camping tents were scattered throughout the park because it was the only park in the city without a curfew. People were dirty from the newspapers they used as blankets. Black, East European, Puerto Rican, Punk Rockers—it seemed everyone had gathered this night to socialize or drink or use the bathroom. Why did they have to be here?

I knew the answer: the shelter system in New York at that time was overwhelmed and unsafe. Besides, many folks who went to shelters were jumped or robbed. There was need everywhere. Churches were overwhelmed; the welfare agencies were overwhelmed; I was overwhelmed. As I walked the seven blocks back to our apartment, probably thirty people asked me for help. Where was my family?

The apartment was empty, so I raced back to the church. But then a strange thing occurred: instead of panic, Isaiah 61:4 came to mind: "They will rebuild the ancient ruins and restore the places long devastated; they will renew the ruined cities that have been devastated for generations." Everywhere I looked, I saw the devastation and the ruin. Yet in the midst, I knew God was somehow present. God was alive and real and working, in spite of my fear. A gust of peace calmed my heart; and as I turned the corner, I saw Susan with our sons in front of the church, smiling and laughing with the neighbors. They were fine. They had simply walked over on a different street to "explore the neighborhood," Susan explained. I had worried for nothing.

My wife and sons were relaxed and enjoying their new community and, in so doing, had already begun to "rebuild the ancient ruins." It was an image I'd return to often over the next few years.

Learning to Trust

Before long, the summer heat turned to winter cold. I spent the six months following our July arrival getting educated in street life and abandoned buildings—not the type of pastoral visits I was used to in California. I listened to stories of muggings at homeless shelters, knife fights with teenagers, and drunken rages from angry boyfriends—not the kind of counseling sessions I was expecting. The Lower East Side of New York City was indeed a different world, and many days I felt completely at a loss. The people who were coming to our Bible studies brought with them a score of personal problems, from mental illnesses I knew little of to violent tempers that sometimes scared the daylights out of me. Their inner struggles were not very conceptual. They were desperate. "How can Christ get me through the day?" "How can Christ help me not to drink, or to get an apartment, or be safe from someone who is threatening me?" "How will I eat?" They were hurt, abused, hopeless, angry, or terrified, and the only thing I knew to expect from them was that they were full of surprises—and needs.

On the other hand, I must confess that I found these people interesting and inspiring. On most of the good days, my heart sang from being here. I remembered reading in high school about the Beat poet Jack Kerouac. (In fact, many of the Beat poets I had read about used to live in a building right next to our storefront.) Kerouac wrote in the 1950s about how he would "just follow bums around" because of their nomadic, countercultural life.

Although the poet and I had different values, I understood what he meant. In some ways, the people I now ministered to were like pilgrims on a quest—they'd given up everything, for whatever reason, and were trying hard to make the best of their circumstances. Even when friends or family asked me what I was doing with "those people," or when I wondered the same thing, I never thought about leaving. No matter how hard it got or how bizarre the interactions were, for some reason leaving just never occurred to me.

I remember one particular September night as we held our weekly Bible study. We were running a meals program and a Bible study, hoping both would help us build relationships in the community before we tried any bigger ministries. Though autumn had officially arrived, we were still feeling the effects of a very hot summer. This particular night, about fifteen or so folks had walked off the streets and into our little storefront for what was sure to be another lively discussion—hopefully about the Bible. We pulled chairs into a circle and tried to cope with the fact that we had no windows for a breeze and no air conditioning to cool us off. If we didn't move much, I told our friends, the flies would probably leave us alone. I picked up a hymnal and turned to number 368.

"That's hymn number 893 if you've got your hymnbook upside down," Bill chimed in. He was a tall African American man who lived across the street in a corner of the abandoned building. Bill had befriended me the first week I was here, showing me the places to avoid, helping me find my way around, introducing me to neighbors. I liked his vibrant take on life, even though I didn't always understand it.

"Hmm. That's true, Bill," I said, staring at him and not quite making the connection. I watched the others flip front and back through the book, as if the pages were a fan. After about five minutes and a few frustrated outbursts, we finally had all turned to the same page.

Lori, our cook, played a tiny electric piano we had set up in the corner, and we mumbled our way through hymn 368 (or 893, depending on your perspective). Victor, a man with a scraggly beard and a fake rubber nose, got up and began to dance slowly, hitting his head with a tambourine as we sang. With each verse, our circle got louder and noisier until Lori hit the final chord and everyone slammed the hymnals closed.

"OK," I announced, "now we are going to have some meditation time before we read the Bible."

"Medication time!" Bill and some of the others shouted. The tambourine man seemed pleased.

"Right," I sighed. After a moment of relative silence, shuffles, and coughs, I suggested we turn in our Bibles to Proverbs 3:5–6. "It's on page 347, in the middle of the Bible. You don't have to turn to it. You can just listen if you want. Maybe someone next to you can help you find it if you need them to." The heat was stifling, and within seconds the study headed down its usual course—into chaos.

Bill fumbled through his Bible. "Proverbs, Proverbs . . . ," he mumbled as he continued turning the pages. "That's what I hate about these new translations. You can never find anything in them." At least he was trying, and I admired his tenacity.

Ms. Turner, a plump pale woman who lived in an abandoned building on Ninth Street and had a reputation as a vicious squatter landlord, said sweetly, "I think Proverbs is one of the most important books in the Bible." I knew her son. He was fourteen, looked like he was twenty-five, and hung around the squatter buildings. I don't think he ever went to any one school for more than a few weeks.

"Don't be reactionary," Brandon scolded her from across the circle. "I've studied all of the religious books of the main religions. Proverbs is a storehouse of capitalistic oppression. Everyone knows that!" Brandon had a dark complexion and curly black hair that flew around his head like dark flames. His eyes blazed with passion as he continued: "I ought to know. I used to work for the Symbionese Liberation Army. I was the editor of a radical newspaper. We're going to take over the neighborhood!" Brandon spit out his words like bullets. Ms. Turner's reputed character began surfacing, and she glared at Brandon with cold cruelty.

"Wait a minute; wait a minute," I pleaded. "Let's at least read the verse before we get started! Who would like to read?" A thin young woman we knew as Jean raised her hand. I nodded and smiled at her, wiping the moisture from my glasses. Jean read the verse slowly, as if each word presented a challenge to her.

"Trust . . . in . . . the . . . LORD . . . with . . . all . . . your . . . um, heart . . . and . . . lean . . . not . . . on . . . um, your . . . own . . . understanding. . . ."

I looked at my watch. By the time she finished reading, the meaning of the passage had escaped everyone.

"That's exactly the kind of verse I'm talking about," Brandon hollered. "It's reactionary. Who can trust anyone?"

"This is about a relationship with God, you idiot," Ms. Turner spat out with true venom.

"Wait a minute; wait a minute," I raised my hands like a referee. "Let's let someone else talk." Sweat poured down my face. "Jean, what do you think 'Trust in the LORD with all your heart' means?"

"Well, my question is this," Jean spoke softly, still choosing her words slowly. She leaned forward and looked me in the eye with childlike earnestness: "What about vomit?"

I stared blankly at her, nodding my head and trying to appear thoughtful. I wiped my forehead again and waited for an explanation from Jean. None came. Neither did a breeze.

"Well, that's an interesting question, Jean," I gulped. "It brings us right back to what we're looking at. Jesus once talked about spewing, literally, vomiting us out if we are lukewarm. Maybe that has something to do with trusting God with *all* your heart."

"Vomiting may be a part of a government conspiracy," Brandon volunteered with great energy. "They've kept us from knowing about the flying saucers that have been visiting our planet for fifty years. They've introduced the AIDS virus into our neighborhood and promulgated a false rumor about where it started. Soon they will work with real estate parasites to close the park on some false pretense and run out all the true residents of the neighborhood."

Another homeless young man who had his bicycle leaning against his lap spoke rapidly, "I'm a true Gnostic, myself. I only read the Gospel of Thomas. All other texts are anti-Semitic."

"What?" four or five people grunted. I groped desperately, trying to find some direction, praying for some kind of intervention, anything.

"But what do you think this sentence means?" I was drowning.

"I think it means how you live," Ms. Turner said quietly. Everyone turned and stared at her. A silent tension hung in the room.

"What do you mean, 'how you live'?" Brandon exploded. "You hire people to beat up squatters with a tire iron when they don't pay you. You make them bleed! You think you're so good, but you buy into the real estate people's plans! You'll help them close the park!"

Ms. Turner's face turned into a wash of fury as she retaliated: "You're nothing but a blood-sucking pagan! I'm not staying in the same room with you!" She stood up and pushed over her chair as if to punctuate her point. Bill picked it up, put it back into the circle, and waited quietly. He seemed to know what was coming.

Then Brandon stood up and crouched behind a chair, eyes bulging. He began to shout obscenities. He looked as though he was ready to spring at Ms. Turner, who by now was shouting even louder. Lori worked calmly on her needlepoint behind the keyboard, as if this were normal for a Wednesday night prayer service.

"Wait a minute; wait a minute." I stood up, too, and made my way to the center of the circle. At the same time, Ms. Turner stomped out of the storefront, still shouting at the "pagan." Brandon stalked around the room, eyeing her and crouching like a leopard.

"That's me," the man with the bike said. "That's me. I don't know what they're talking about."

"OK, OK," I said. Brandon lurked by the piano. "Let's try again next week. I'll say a prayer." It was the most feeble, disheartened prayer ever uttered, I was sure. Why had I taken this job again? What if I decided to pursue something else that wasn't quite so . . . weird? But Lori interrupted my fantasy by suggesting everyone have some coffee and "calm down." I mumbled something about a good idea and began talking to some of the group, leaving Brandon by the portable piano to cool off.

As we talked and drank coffee, a woman I hadn't met yet came up to me. She was clean and well dressed, and looked me in the eye. She spoke gently.

"I want you to know I will support you as you try to do your Bible study. I know it can be difficult with some of these people."

I admitted needing all the help I could get and was relieved that someone rational understood my challenge. Then my spirit began to rise, and I confessed to this new friend that I was feeling very inadequate at this "type" of ministry, not certain what direction I should take. Maybe God had sent her just to encourage me on this September night.

We talked for several more minutes while most of the group chatted or wandered back into the street. I was thankful for at least one person in the Bible study that night who wasn't shouting or talking about vomit or Gnosticism. Everything she said was purposeful and reasonable.

"I live down the street and will be back for the next Bible study," she said to me, smiling. I thanked her for her support; and then all of a sudden, she opened her eyes as wide as saucers and blurted, "You see, I get most of my information from a deer on the highway, who sends signals through car headlights to one of my knees."

What did she say?

She narrowed her eyes, leaned in toward me, and whispered, "But the old man in the apartment below me is trying to intercept these messages."

I looked at her for a long second, took a big slow gulp of my coffee, and said, "Uh, huh. I see." I stood next to Bill for the rest of the night.

As I walked home that night, I was not sure if anything good had come from our Wednesday night Bible study. Had anyone even heard the Scriptures? Did anyone learn anything about Jesus? Was any of the Bible study even worthwhile? I had no answers. But as I walked up the steps of our apartment, I suddenly had a whole new appreciation of what it meant to "trust in the LORD with all your heart, and lean not on your own understanding." Because if I *was* sure about anything, it was that I did not understand these people this night, leaving me little choice but to trust in the Lord with all my heart. I said a silent prayer for help. And as I did, I heard a little song jump out of my soul and into my voice. The melody of the hymn about trust that we sang earlier came back to me, and I was humming by the time I unlocked the front door.

The Lower East Side felt a little more like where I was supposed to be.

> *The world is coming to a new beginning.*
> —GRAFFITI ON THE WALL OF
> OUR STOREFRONT CHURCH

chapter three
Sanctuary of Hope

The next few months turned into a year; and before we knew it, we were celebrating our first anniversary at Graffiti Baptist Ministry. Most of our days were filled with what we called "relationship building." We wanted to get to know the people as friends and try to establish a sense of trust and safety. By offering lunches and clothing to our homeless neighbors around Tompkins Square Park, running tutoring programs and vacation Bible schools for kids in the community, and, of course, continuing our always interesting Wednesday Bible study, I expected relationships would be built, lives transformed, and God's purposes quickly fulfilled.

I had a lot more to learn.

That fact became more and more obvious to me whenever we were asked what we were doing in *this* neighborhood, working with *these* people. To be honest, in some of those early days, I also found myself wondering what we were doing. When people would question me about our work, I'd mumble, "Uh, well, it's a . . . a ministry." I couldn't quite say the word *church* yet, especially because we were just a little group of people in the Lower East Side of Manhattan, bound together from very different backgrounds and with various threads of need and worship.

Besides, a few years before, I had tried serving as an interim pastor at what for me was a more familiar kind of church, a supportive suburban congregation, but my wife and I were not sure that what we had to offer was what they needed. We also knew that we weren't called to overseas missionary work, although we had appreciated our time teaching in Hong Kong. No, we had come to the Lower East Side because we saw a need, because we loved New York City, and because we had what I've heard referred to as "an inner sense of oughtness." That is, the ministry through Graffiti is what we felt called by God to do, what we *ought* to do. Frederick Buechner talks about *vocation* as "the place where your deep gladness and the world's deep hunger meet."* Once we found out the position at Graffiti was open, it simply never occurred to us to be anywhere else. As we prayerfully made the decision, Susan and I knew we wanted to be here; seeing how God opened the doors for us was a thrill.

Maybe our feeling of commitment was also due in part to the deep respect we felt toward the people who had helped establish Graffiti Ministries long before we arrived. In 1974, a seminary student and other people from various Baptist churches began by helping neighborhood children learn how to read. When the group of faithful Christians first began dreaming

---

*Frederick Buechner, *Wishful Thinking* (New York: Harper and Row Publishers, 1973), 95.

about ministering on the Lower East Side, they had looked for a building or space to work from. They hunted diligently for the right space until one day they discovered what they thought was the perfect spot in an abandoned storefront on East Seventh Street. The only problem was that several bulky motor-cycle gang members already lived there. The gang had taken over the former porn shop, had painted the storefront room black, and were now keeping their bikes safely inside.

Legend has it that one gutsy gray-haired woman marched right into the storefront full of bikers and politely asked, "Would you gentlemen please leave? We would like to teach children how to read here." I can only imagine her standing there, like Daniel in the lion's den, facing off with a roomful of big hairy guys who stared back at her with their mouths open. I'm sure they had never before seen anything like her.

Apparently it worked. Shortly after her confrontation, they moved to another storefront around the corner. Then a college student work team from Alabama came in to make the place presentable. Each time they'd paint over the graffiti that covered the outside of the storefront, the graffiti would mysteriously return to the walls the very next day. Finally some genius in the group said, "Why fight it? Jesus Christ can be a message written on the wall too. Let's call the place 'Graffiti' and put our own message on the neighborhood."

Residents, I was told, were astonished to see the enthusias-tic students working on the littered street surrounded by aban-doned buildings, painting the little storefront with a new kind of graffiti. The wall was soon covered with a jazzy flurry of writing, letters, and colors overlapping and crammed together. In one small corner someone neatly wrote: "The world is coming to a new beginning."

Since then, of course, everyone in the neighborhood has known the place as "Graffiti," no matter how many well-intentioned church folks have tried to change the name. Many more work teams have come through the doors to help us carry on the original vision of this Baptist mission, but sometimes no amount of help or history prepares you for the new beginnings that wait for you around the corner.

Running for Cover

"There's some guy here from the denominational office to see you," my coworker shouted from upstairs. The visitor wore a dark suit and tie, held a brown leather briefcase in his hand, and every hair on his head was in place as he waited for me in our office. I smiled awkwardly as I greeted him, shook his hand, and suggested we walk down the street to get some coffee.

Not many men in suits and ties walked through our neighborhood. Still, I pretended not to notice as I wiped my brow and commented on the weather. This was our first official visit from someone from the denominational office. He told me he was here simply to observe the ministry and to see if there was any way he could help. His voice was clear and sincere, and I felt a little calmer as I listened.

That is, until he surveyed the park, turned to me, and asked, "Are there any drugs here?" No sooner had the words popped out of his mouth than a hypodermic needle landed on the sidewalk inches in front of us. We both jumped at least three feet backward. The well-groomed worker gasped in disbelief. But I was even more upset since it had almost hit me in the head. Never mind what this official was thinking; I suddenly had visions of returning home to my wife and sons wearing a Lower East Side hypodermic beanie.

"Someone must have been using heroin up there," I said, trying to sound matter-of-fact as I pointed to some open windows several stories above. "Once they finished their business, they must have just tossed the needle out the window," I shrugged. My denominational friend seemed a little less sure of himself as we walked the rest of the way to the diner. As we sat down in a booth, I uttered a silent prayer: "Lord, keep me from saying something stupid."

"I often don't know what I'm doing, and I feel as though there is always a crisis," I said as we sat at the table. "I think about how foolish the disciples must have felt as Jesus gave them bits of five hamburger buns and two sardines. My new motto is: Start with what you've got, just like Jesus told his disciples to do. They faced overwhelming needs of hunger and lostness too." The visitor didn't say anything.

After we drank our coffee and talked about ministry strategies, I decided to walk my visitor to one side of the park. I thought this might be a harmless way of introducing him to the neighborhood, allowing him to get a glimpse of some of the things we had just been discussing. What I didn't know was that the police had descended on the park by the time we arrived; they were trying to remove some people who had built tiny shelters out of cardboard and mattresses in between park benches. The police were standing in a circle around the area, and the residents of the small structures were running back and forth between the huts, shouting all sorts of things at the police. The eyes of my suit-and-tie visitor grew big.

Suddenly, I saw smoke rising from one of the huts that had been covered with a plastic sheet. The newspaper and cardboard inside were dry and provided perfect fuel for the fire. Flames shot fifteen feet into the air. In an instant, another hut went up in flames. Then another. The people in the park were so angry the police were trying to dislocate them that they had begun to actually set their own possessions on fire!

Everything in the neighborhood seemed to be crumbling. More structures were set on fire; more curse words were thrown at the police. By now we were rushing through the park, fires on each side of us, smoke rising high through the park trees; I felt as if I were in someone's nightmare. When I looked through the smoke, I could see people coming out of the expensive condominiums across the street. Those people were also well-dressed, but to my amazement, they hardly seemed to notice the fires or the folks who were burning their own meager possessions. Instead, they were just trying to get a taxi. I thought about the interesting contrast: people with everything right next to people with nothing, and I wondered if my visitor had noticed the same.

"This is like Calcutta, where you're either really rich or really poor," my denominational friend said. "People who have so very much walk right by people who have so very little."

The fire department arrived and seemed to get things under control. We were "encouraged" to move along. As we walked back to the office, trying to make sense of what we had just witnessed, Sam—my shaggy-haired friend with the butcher knife—intercepted us.

"You don't have a butcher knife in that bag, do you, Sam?" I teased Sam now as my denominational friend glanced from my face to Sam's and back again. This had probably not been a typical visit for him.

"No, no, no," Sam said earnestly. "I've got an iron bar now, as long as a baseball bat." I introduced Sam to my friend, and both nervously shook the other's hand. Then Sam took me aside for a moment and told me he wanted to share something in the next Bible study, but he said, "I'm a little scared. I don't know if I can do it. It's a prayer. I took it from that 'The-Lord-is-my-shepherd' verse. Here's how it goes: 'Oh Lord, you're the shepherd and I'm the sheep. I sure hope you're a vegetarian—'"

Sam fell out laughing. His sense of humor really did qualify him to be an urban comedian. I bit my lip and nodded my head to Sam, trying to encourage him. By this time our visitor from the denominational office said he had to get going, so I told Sam I'd see him later that week. He smiled at me as if he understood my dilemma. "No problem, man, see ya," he hollered after us, still chuckling to himself.

I tried explaining to our visitor that one of the great aspects of living here was that I had begun to see God work through weakness, through people I would never have expected, and in completely unexpected ways. He nodded his head in agreement and listened with compassion. He placed his hand on my shoulder and said a prayer for me before he walked toward the subway. I couldn't help wondering how he would describe our visit.

But I hardly had time to worry. By the time I got back to the office, George was sitting on the stoop with a young couple. George was a young dark-haired man who had lived on the streets for nine years; he had run away from home when he was thirteen and had lived in abandoned buildings in the Lower East Side most of the time since. He had ordered his "ordination papers" from the back of a magazine, but I don't think he ever received them. Still, somewhere along the way he had found a priest's collar he liked to wear. People often thought he was a "man of the cloth" and, consequently, poured out their woes to him. George loved to live up to their expectations by lending a hand in any way he could, and he drank up the attention.

Once he saw me, though, he excused himself from his "counseling session" and approached me with genuine concern. The color in his face started fading, and I knew George was upset.

"It's got to be soon," he announced to me with desperation. "I can't stay in that building much longer, Taylor. The junkies are on the bottom floor. I found a dead body there last week. Can you believe it? I just can't take it. If I get a place, will you help me move? Can you get a van or something? I've got a lot of valuable stuff up there."

I tried hard to imagine what George had just told me. His eyes were clouding, and I was in awe—again—at the things that people endured. Sometimes I felt George was pompous and self-serving, but I admired his will to survive and his childlike earnestness. I felt protective of him, too, like a father for a son.

"Slow down, George. Take a breath. Now tell me again what's happening." George sat back on the stoop and repeated his story, this time with greater emotion. As much as he had tried to get off the street, George's only refuge had been an abandoned building on Avenue D, which wasn't really an abandoned building because so many "residents"—junkies, alcoholics, runaways, stray cats—were living there. Months before, he had applied for housing with the city but was put on a waiting list like the hundreds of other friends in our neighborhood. Every time he tried to call to see if he'd qualified yet, he merely received bureaucratic answers. Now George's patience was wearing thin.

I walked toward Avenue D with this young man, as he waved in a priestly fashion to every needy-looking human who walked past us. I forced a smile and tried to talk with George about some possible solutions. He all but ignored me, waving like a visiting dignitary until we reached the boarded-up building where he lived.

The tenement was like most of the other buildings in the area. It had a fire escape on the front and towered six or seven stories high, but this one had cinderblocks in the spots where there should have been windows. Unlike the building next to it that was nicely painted and had lace curtains hanging behind glass windows, this place looked as neglected as the people whom George told me lived inside. Some of the windows on the higher floors had plywood over them. Other windows were blackened, opened spaces, like missing teeth on a man beaten.

The attempts by the city to seal the building and keep people from entering had been feeble. Someone had knocked out the sealed doorway and installed a door that they had found on the street. A heavy chain hung from the doorknob hole in the door, though it wasn't locked. George entered quickly.

I followed the "priest" through the makeshift doorway. Inside, my senses were immediately overcome with darkness and the smell of urine and cats. I looked around and saw a few small shafts of light coming through the walls. It was cold and dank. I shivered, feeling like I was falling into a cave. Then I heard rustling noises around me, a startling change from the busy street noises outside. I felt George's flannel shirt in front of me and obeyed when he told me to "hang onto the wall," a dirty, wet wall with peeling paint that would lead me to his home. I heard faint voices, coughs, and an occasional curse word, and I wondered about the likelihood of getting mugged or stabbed by any of these down-on-your-luck characters. But it was too late to leave; I was in their territory, George's territory.

My mind went wild. The place was like a Gothic cathedral that had been bombed during a war and never restored; it had no electricity, no running water, no hint of God. It was just another burned-out building with burned-out people living in it, I thought, a metaphor for the neighborhood of all that was wrong with the city. Here, buildings and people alike were shells, the result of both a society that had abandoned them and a heart of sin that led them toward decay.

A million thoughts flew through my mind. Maybe we should start an abandoned building outreach. Maybe we should rehabilitate these buildings to make affordable housing without pushing out the people who live here. Maybe we should put together an AIDS awareness seminar for these strung-out folks. Of course, then I wondered what junkie shooting up is going to remember to come to an AIDS seminar?

George's whisper recaptured my attention, and I took small cautious steps behind him. Everything around me was dirty and blackened; it looked as though there had been several fires inside. Splintered wood and peeling plaster hung from the ceiling and walls. I now understood why George was so desperate to get out.

He went to the stairs without looking around, and I followed him. As I turned the corner, I glanced through an open door into a back room. There were at least fifteen filthy mattresses and old futons strewn across the floor. The room was in semi-darkness except for one golden shaft of light from a window that wasn't boarded up. Thin, motionless bodies were lying on some of the mattresses. It was as still as a graveyard.

"Who lives there?" I asked as we climbed the stairs to George's place.

"I'll tell you later," George said as he moved as quickly as he could. For once, he acted as though he didn't want to talk to anyone.

When we got to his floor, George unlocked the padlock on the chain that kept the door shut. The noise of the chain rattled down the empty hallway. As we entered, the smell of cats was stronger than it had been when we first came into the building below. Two skinny cats sitting on a pile of charred wood looked at us suspiciously and darted off.

"It's hard to keep things clean here," George said, moving things around as if he were tidying. "The plumbing's out. I have to use the bathroom in a plastic bucket and carry it down the stairs. I have to carry water up too. It's hard. Now, what you saw downstairs was what they call a shooting gallery." George began to talk more officially, as if he were a tour guide. "That's where the junkies come and shoot up. That's why I can't stay here any longer. It's disgusting."

He was right; the place was filthy. A thick film of dirt covered everything in his tiny room. I looked at the shopping cart in the middle of the room.

"I burn wood in there to stay warm," my friend told me. Then I listened as George shared with me his dream of getting a real apartment, a place where he could bring friends if they needed a safe place to crash, a warm home with a toilet and a shower and maybe even a stove. George liked to cook. I nodded and walked into the adjoining room. My eyes became fixed on another dirty wall that to my shock had the Lord's Prayer neatly painted across it.

"I did that," George beamed. He read it for me there in the semidarkness of this filthy corner of a boarded-up building. He folded his hands as he recited it. I listened, suddenly very aware of how little I had endured in life compared to the presence standing before me.

"Yes, George, I guess we can get a van to help you when the time comes," I whispered, hoping it would be sooner than later. A soft smile spread across George's face, and he patted my shoulder in thanks. Then he locked his room and led me back outside into the sunlight.

Before that day, I would never have thought that a person like George—living in an abandoned building—would reach out to others by encouraging them or offering them a place to sleep. But that is what he did a few months later when the housing authorities finally called him and told him his day had come. We moved his belongings into what he called his "Sanctuary of Hope," a small studio apartment that was just like the place he had dreamed of. He even made a business card with his name and address and the words "Sanctuary of Hope" at the top. And sure enough, George kept wearing his priest's collar and invited friends home to stay with him. George had known failure and pain most of his life, yet he never hesitated to reach out and serve someone else. I would have thought that someone like George would have been so focused on his own pain that he would not have thought of another's. Later, George was thrown out of his apartment by a couple he allowed to stay with him. He lived in an abandoned synagogue the next winter before he got his apartment back. Still, he never lost hope.

I was never quite sure how God was going to use these people to help me confront my own weaknesses and to encourage the other friends in the neighborhood. I began to notice when they refused to have self-pity and how often they exhibited a depth of generosity I had never experienced. Of course, there were also some very strange and quirky sides to some of the folks. Still, that didn't seem to matter as much because with each passing month I was seeing their growth. And in the process, I was seeing my own as well.

Real Communion

By 1989, we were taking Bill and Sam and several others from our Wednesday night Bible study to our mother church in midtown each Sunday. Although the congregation there was extremely kind and welcoming to us, Susan and the other Graffiti staff members and I were growing increasingly uncomfortable taking our little group of wild kids and colorful adults from the Lower East Side to the different world of this midtown Baptist church. The more we talked, the more we realized we needed our own Sanctuary of Hope, a safe place where friends could feel comfortable. We needed to start a church.

At first, Sunday morning worship services were slow to catch on, but soon Graffiti Church services were as interesting as our Wednesday night Bible studies, albeit in a different way. We sang hymns, prayed together, took Communion in paper cups, listened to Scripture readings and church announcements, and on good days, I'd even make it through an entire sermon without too many interruptions. Although people sometimes took the opportunity to catch up on their sleep, mostly they came to be together and to hear about God's hope. We were becoming a church.

One Sunday morning, though, as my family and I stepped out of our apartment and into the February chill, I could feel the bitter air penetrate my bones. I was tired. Programs had been busy, and work had been demanding. I looked around the snowy block and held my sons close to me as we walked toward East

Seventh Street. Was it only a few years ago that I had left Susan and the boys with her parents while I found an apartment for us in this neighborhood? Where had the time gone?

The Lower East Side was radically different from San Francisco, but we were settling in, and I was certainly learning a lot. That morning as we hurried through the cold—past closed-up bars, old tenement buildings, and along the park—I suddenly felt my attitude change and my energy come back. I thought about how significant this Sunday morning would be for those of us at Graffiti Church. Though we were just a small Christian family, made up mostly of friends who weren't always sure where they lived or what they believed, we were a pretty honest bunch. Tired as I was, I loved these folks.

And this particular Sunday, I was especially excited to see their faces. Why? This morning we were moving from the world of Dixie cups and paper plates to a real Communion set to celebrate the Lord's Supper. Our mother church in midtown had given us a new brass-plated set, and I was sure our members would be pleased. Besides, I had prepared an important sermon discussing Paul's letter to the Ephesians, dealing specifically with what it meant for Christians to be the church. I was sure we were in for a special worship service.

What I hadn't yet learned, however, was that what you expect or hope will happen in urban ministry rarely does. Rebuilding the ancient ruins—like Isaiah 61:4 says—is not often black and white.

When we arrived at Graffiti, friends and neighbors from the streets were finding their way in out of the cold. I almost ran into Clara, a spicy older woman with white hair that matched her skin. Clara used to live in Central Park with her husband, but they had worked hard to find a tiny room of their own in a building a few blocks away. She was shivering from the cold, and I wondered how she held up in times like these.

"Clara, good to see you. Will you help us pass out Communion this morning?" I asked, resting my hand on her shoulder.

"Why not?" she shrugged. "Just show me what to do. I've never done it before." Clara's face wrinkled with determination, as if this was one of life's greater challenges. She rubbed her hands and took her seat near the front.

I waved as George (always the priest) and Sam (with his bulging bag) hurried through the door and found a chair. Then I noticed that Roy had walked in. He wore a huge dark coat and about ten layers of shirts and pants underneath it. Someone directed him to a seat by the heater so he could warm up.

"I feel a little loquacious this morning." That was Roy's favorite word—*loquacious.* "I've been standing with the guys around the garbage can in the park. They've got a fire going pretty good there, but I have got to watch my health. They put some varnished boards or something in there. I don't think it's good for you." Roy grumbled his words out in a low, throaty voice, and I noticed no one in particular was listening to him.

"That's fine, Roy. Have a seat," I tried to encourage him.

"OK, everybody sit down. Now!" announced Bill. His rich, booming voice demanded respect, and I admired his natural ability. And with that, the service began. First, we screeched out a couple of hymns, though Bill did a pretty good job of keeping us on pitch. Someone said a prayer. A few people staggered in late and shuffled to their chairs. One of them was a woman I knew as Faith, a soft-spoken lady with matted brown hair and lots of plastic bags beside her.

Announcements were made, and then it was my time—my time to preach.

"The letter to the Ephesians has a lot to say about church," I proclaimed.

Roy with his ten layers of clothing began to settle down and looked sleepy.

I continued: "Paul in this letter first says God's plan is to reconcile all things through Christ. All things."

Clara adjusted the glasses in the new Communion set.

"But according to Scripture, the church is like a pilot project for what God wants to do."

Faith, with the matted hair, began to pick through the braids behind her ear.

"As God unites us through Christ in our weakness here, we show God's multicolored wisdom to all the principalities and powers. In the Bible, weakness is the envelope for God's power."

Faith had found something. She held it between her thumb and first finger and began to examine it. My train of thought was waning.

"As churches multiply, there are more and more places of healing," I continued.

Faith flicked the insect at Clara. Clara, who never had a really long fuse, jumped up in anger, snorted, and carried the Communion set to the other side of the room. People began to shift in their seats. A bald spot in our little group began to appear around Faith.

"We know church is important." I was reaching. "The letter to the Ephesians says Christ loves the church and gave himself for her."

Then Bill passed me a note in the middle of my sermon. Scrawled across the wrinkled page was this message: "There must be a gas leak in here! I smell something funny." I looked at the note and continued to preach, though I knew I had good reason to believe my friend's warning. I tried to breathe in through my nose without being too noticeable. A strong, chemical smell hung in the air, and by now I had totally lost my train of thought.

"We'll talk more about church later. Now we will quickly move to the partaking of the Lord's Supper." I began to have visions of the entire storefront blowing up before we finished the service.

Carefully, we unveiled our new Communion set. I said a few words, and Clara began to carry the gilded plate with bread on it to the people sitting throughout the room. This was our first Communion with a real Communion set, and I was thrilled. Roy even looked up from his nap and admired the golden plate before closing his eyes again.

As she walked toward the center aisle, Clara stubbed her toe on the first chair and almost dropped the whole set. "S——!" she shouted. No one noticed.

So much for liturgical reverence, I thought. By this time, the chemical smell was becoming stronger and stronger. We finished the Lord's Supper, and I said the fastest closing prayer I had ever uttered.

After a chorus of "Amens," I asked our small congregation to rise.

"Let's all join hands and get in a circus," I said, using my most pastoral voice. "I mean circle." Then I announced that there was a possible gas leak in the building and that we needed to move quickly. Roy, whose eyes were still closed, began to shift uneasily in his seat as the group of people moved faster than I'd ever seen them, out of the storefront and up the stairs into the tiny apartment above.

I ran toward the phone and called the gas company. Within minutes the gas company people came and checked our gas pipes. We waited and chatted over coffee and snores. When the gas man walked into the apartment, Bill, Clara, Susan, and the rest turned their heads. Anticipation filled the room.

"There's no leak," the gas man said routinely, and he walked down the stairs and out of the building. The chemical smell began to recede.

What would we do now? I followed the man downstairs. When I returned, all of a sudden I noticed the chemical smell again! I looked at the person sleeping in the chair next to the heater. It was Roy. Then I understood. Roy had been trying to keep warm and had spent the early morning standing in the cold next to a trash can that was on fire. They must have been burning something that had been strongly chemical. As Roy strolled into our storefront and began to warm up, the smell from his clothes permeated the room.

I may be the only pastor in the country this Sunday who cut short the morning service because of the smell of one of my members, I thought.

"There's no gas leak," I announced as I walked upstairs. "Everyone have some coffee. I'll finish my sermon on Christ and the church next week."

"Good idea, Pastor," someone said. "But it was a real nice Communion."

I smiled at the warm weathered faces of Bill and these other friends and thought about their circumstances, their homes, their hearts. As if God himself was whispering in my ear, I realized *we* were the church, needy and different, desperate and helpful. That Sunday morning service might have been the first time I began to thank the Lord for how much he was using these people in this place to show me more than I ever could have imagined.

As I sipped my coffee, I heard a soft, but sure, song about trust once again rising in my heart. And I knew—in spite of sweltering heat or bitter cold—that I was in the right place.

Didn't Jesus wear high-top sandals,
all the way up to his knees?
—FAITH, AT OUR BIBLE STUDY

c h a p t e r
f o u r
Nontraditional Values

A few months after our first "real" Communion, Susan and I
found a new apartment around the corner and a half block farther from the church. Instead of the fourth-floor walk-up of our
first hot summer here, we were excited to find a two-bedroom
apartment on the first floor of a building that was probably a
hundred years old. Of course, I'd seen pastors' offices bigger
than the bedrooms in our new place, but we were grateful to
have an apartment like this that we could afford in the neighborhood. To make the most of our limited space, a few kind
work teams built loft beds and ladders for our sons in their
room and put their desks underneath, similar to the loft
already in the other bedroom. We got used to looking through
the thick metal bars outside our living room windows to see
the barbed wire fences surrounding our building. And we

didn't really mind that it took three keys in three different locks just to come into the building and our apartment. We knew we had more than most of our friends in this neighborhood, and each day it was getting easier for us to call this home.

One night shortly after we moved in, the phone rang. I stepped over boxes scattered throughout our living room to answer the phone and heard the familiar voice of my older brother, Robin. He was calling from his suburban California home to see how we liked our new apartment. Since moving from Oklahoma—he and his wife to the West Coast and Susan and I to the East—he had made a point of calling me once a week just to check in and catch up. (He still does to this day.) Though my brother and I don't share the same Christian faith, he's always been supportive of me. He's one of the happiest, most positive men I know.

But that doesn't mean he's always understood our decisions. Considering that he and his wife have been hard-working doctors, Robin was a little uncertain of what to make of our decision to head up Graffiti Ministries. In fact, I still remember when we first told him we were coming to the Lower East Side. With big-brother concern, he was both puzzled and respectful of our decisions. He was interested in why I, as a Ph.D., would bring my family to *this* neighborhood when I might be teaching in a university or doing some other work. But if this was our direction, he would support us, he said. That acceptance wasn't easy for him, though, especially because his particular fondness for his two nephews often made him question whether raising them in the city was a good idea. The phone call this night was also to see how the boys were doing with the move. I smiled at the tone of his voice and his questions.

"I'm so proud of Freeman," I told my brother. "He's fine with the new place, and he's the only kid in his kindergarten program who can read!"

"If you keep him in those public schools, when he's sixteen, he'll still be the only kid in his class who can read," my brother commented morosely. Though I knew he was joking, I could hear the concern in his voice.

"I know, I know; they're not having the kind of childhood you and I had," I responded to my brother as I settled into the couch. "I don't like it either that on the way to school the other day, Freeman picked up something on the sidewalk and asked me what it was. It was a hypodermic needle, and I thought, *What am I doing here?* I know it doesn't have the fresh air and the sports that we had in Oklahoma, Robin, but I think he and Owen [our other son] are doing OK. Besides, Freeman's developing his own urban skills."

"Like what?" Robin waited.

"Well, he may not be able to milk a cow, but he can sure hail a cab! And Owen loves New York. When we came back from vacation on the plane, he ran to the water fountain in the airport, took a big drink, and said, 'Ahhh, taste the lead in the water!' Remember our family reunion in Oklahoma, when there were all those doughnuts spread out on the table? Freeman ran up to Susan and gushed, 'Mom, these are the best bagels I've ever eaten!' The boys are doing all right. Really."

"That's my point, Taylor," Robin's voice was stern now. "They're doing all right, but are you sure that place is best for them?"

The words stung for a moment. It wasn't as if his question was new to me. More than once I had faced the reality that my brother earned a lot of money, while we were earning a mission pastor's salary. He'd achieved high status in a meaningful job, and we were working in one of the poorest congressional districts in the New York City area. What kind of Ph.D. would be here in this place? My sisters, too, were all achievers and had married professional men—a doctor, a pro football player, a construction manager. Sometimes I missed having a professional's income.

Susan and I had wrestled over this issue together as well, but we always seemed to come back to the advantages of being here, to all the opportunities the boys would have. Susan was committed to being at home with our sons, to being involved in their schools or activities. She'd make toys for them out of cardboard boxes or take them on field trips throughout the city to teach them about New York history or to show them God's creativity expressed in the variety of people who live here. She'd become a type of urban pioneer woman, and even though we now lived in a tiny apartment with loft beds, wasn't the most important thing the time that we spent with each other? Plus, Susan always reminded me that this was the work that made my heart sing. As I reasoned thus with myself, I gained strength for the conversation with my brother.

"Just think, Robin, you and I never saw a great, original work of art until we were in our twenties. I'd never seen a Shakespearean play or a symphony until I moved here. My boys see that stuff all the time. Kids don't have to have a lot of big things or a big backyard to have a great childhood. Freeman even wants to be the curator of a museum when he grows up!"

There was silence on the phone. Then my brother decided to change the subject. Though it was not easy for me when we talked about these issues, I knew deep down that Robin respected our decisions. He knew that we were no worse off than someone in the suburbs who worked all the time and rarely took a day off. At least we lived in a neighborhood where I could walk home for lunch when I wanted to and that our family could spend time together.

In fact, in other conversations we'd had, he was quick to recognize that there actually were many advantages to living here, such as the obvious exposure to diversity. In contrast to growing up in our homogenous Oklahoma town, urban living was somewhat color-blind on the Lower East Side. Kids from the earliest grades know who they are in relation to the various ethnic backgrounds. Robin had seen the picture we sent our mom of Owen's kindergarten graduating class, and we told him how much she loved the fact that all the faces were different. Of course, sometimes so much diversity was not easy. Developing a sense of empathy for those who are different can be a challenge, and feeling like a minority often takes its toll. But in urban public schools, at least kids have a chance to engage in discussions with others who are not like them, learning firsthand that the world does not present a level playing field.

"Besides, Robin," I picked up our previous thread of conversation again. "I think we're healthier here. We don't have a car. We walk everywhere. You know as well as I do that the farthest we used to walk is from the living room to the driveway. Sure, we've got smog. Sure, on some summer days it looks like fog as you walk down the street. But, hey man, we've got our street legs. The people in the mission tell me it takes two months to get your street legs. Then you can walk anywhere, no problem. You don't even need the subways anymore."

"All right, all right, you've made your point," my brother said, laughing by this time and informing me that swimming pools were just fine for his exercise, thank you very much.

I laughed as we hung up the phone. Still, I sat in the dark living room for a long time, just thinking. My brother did have a point: sometimes our values clashed, and I realized what a long way we had come. It was interesting to consider that though my brother, sisters, and I all were raised going to church, Robin and I both went through a phase when we decided we wouldn't believe in God. My firm belief at that point was that all life came from "time plus space plus chance," and my older brother was quick to agree. As young college students, we both lived according to that philosophy.

But when we went to Europe to study abroad, I was the one who began to experience a change in what I believed. I had been studying English at Wake Forest University in North Carolina with the intention of going into law. Robin was doing a medical school externship in England, so we traveled together around Europe for a month. With each day of the trip, our discussions grew more intense. He liked to tell me then that positing one unknown to explain another unknown in this world didn't do any good. The more I thought about our lives, however, the more I wasn't so sure I agreed with him. On trains and in youth hostels and cafés across Europe, my brother and I talked often about the meaning of life and our purpose in it.

After Robin left, my year-abroad program took me to Berlin. I was very lonely for the next six months, finally getting so desperate for English that I started reading the New Testament because it was the only book in English I had. Although I hid that New Testament from acquaintances who came to my room as if it had been pornography, I still kept reading it. The words came alive, making more sense than anything else I had ever read. When I returned home, my older sister shared with me how she had been changed by Christ. Even though I pretended not to care, her words affected me deeply, so much so that on my way back to school, in a motel room, I prayed and said, "Christ, if you're there, I want you in my life."

Later, my big brother and I got to a point where he said, "Well, Taylor, if you're right about what you believe, then I guess I'll know it when I die. If I am right, neither of us will know it." Once I became a Christian, we had to recognize that we were coming from radically different places. Although we had to "agree to disagree," we never stopped loving each other.

When I returned to college in Winston Salem, North Carolina, my newfound faith in Christ led me to the Salvation Army Boy's Club, where I worked with youth for a year. Then I decided that instead of law school, I should go to seminary. Princeton Seminary in New Jersey, an hour or so from New York City, introduced me to urban life and social ministry for the first time. I became the youth director at a Baptist church, and by 1978, we started focusing on the youth in, of all places, Harlem. After graduating from Princeton, I went to Golden Gate Baptist Seminary for my Ph.D. as the final step before coming back to New York City and Graffiti. Now I was really a long way from home, and Robin was genuinely concerned. Still, once he realized that I was doing what made my heart sing, that I was doing what I felt called by God to do, then he shrugged his shoulders and offered his support. Of course, it was hard not being near family, but Susan and I knew God had given us a new family, one that came in all colors and backgrounds—our extended family at Graffiti.

My big brother chose a path of hard work, professional competence, and cultural awareness. I, on the other hand, headed down a path that led to people with some altogether different standards, bringing my family to a place that forever prided itself on being a little bit of everything, a place that was anything but traditional. And while I felt I was only trying to bring the values of God's kingdom to our ministry, I don't think I fully realized just how nontraditional life would be during those first few years on the Lower East Side.

Living in the Zoo

Even though our families were far away, Susan and I were learning to love being in New York City. Watching people, human nature at its fullest, always made us feel more alive, making our continuing assimilation to city life easier. We thoroughly understood writer H. L. Menken's response when he was asked why he bothered to live in New York, considering the fact that he always criticized the city.

"Why do people go to zoos?" he'd answer dryly.

Maybe our fascination with the city also had something to do with how we grew up. My brother and I used to sit in grocery store parking lots with our mom in Enid just to watch people as they walked back and forth. He and I did the same sitting together in European cafés. After Susan and I met, we also enjoyed observing the people in each place we lived. One game we played when we were dating was "who on this subway car would you want to be?" It was not difficult transferring our people-watching fascination to New York, especially since there was so much to observe.

On any given day, for instance, I would walk down the street and see someone in pajamas or some wild outfit walking toward me. I loved strolling down First Avenue where you could smell the fish market, the bakery, the flower and fruit stands, the garbage and coffee. Soon—and in spite of the fact that this was a completely different place than any I had known before, a place dogged by persistent needs and strange habits—I found my love for the city growing. I was perpetually amazed at the way people looked, at the smells of life, at the varied colors of skin or hair or clothes. Someone once said that if people were God's treasure, New York City would be the treasure chest. Once we settled into our new apartment, I also began discovering how deep—and costly—that treasure could be. Literally.

One day, after walking through Tompkins Square Park and seeing my usual neighbors sleeping on their benches or in their makeshift shacks, I arrived at the office just in time to hear the buzzer going on and on and on. I set down my backpack and finally got to the intercom. "What is it? What is it?" I shouted.

"It's George! You gotta come down right now. It's an emergency!"

"It's always an emergency," I grumbled as I walked down the stairs to the main floor.

George stood nervously at the bottom of the stairs. As usual, he was wearing his priest's collar, and his wild dark hair looked as if he hadn't combed it for a week. His usually youthful face was heavy and tired as he waited for me to come down to him.

"It's Peggy," he said without any introduction or apologies. "You're going to have to do something as soon as possible." He spoke with an irritating superiority, as if he were my supervisor, even though he was much younger than I, and I tried hard to remember the thing about God's treasure.

"What's the problem, George? And how's your new apartment?" I mumbled, feeling surly and suspicious. Peggy was a woman who ate dinner at our storefront on Wednesdays. To be honest, she looked and smelled like the stereotypical bag lady. In fact, every time I saw her, she was carrying two or three plastic shopping bags stuffed with smaller brown paper bags that were stuffed with who knew what. Although none of us ever found out what was in those brown paper bags, they were apparently so important to Peggy that she would never let them out of her sight. She also loved classic movies and adored Bette Davis. In fact, in a strange sort of way, Peggy actually looked and acted like the old Bette Davis. Most of the time she was congenial and gracious, but every now and then she erupted in accusations. "You poisoned my turkey!" she shouted venomously one Thanksgiving, sending the poor cook off in tears.

"It's her apartment," George said with priestly condescension. "They're going to evict her. You gotta go over there. They say it's all the junk she has in her apartment. The landlord just wants her out! That's all it is!" George paced the area at the base of our stairs, genuinely concerned for his friend. He wasn't particularly close to Peggy, but he understood from firsthand experience the pain of being evicted and what happened when one suddenly ended up homeless. He was right about one thing: something had to be done.

I had often wondered whether Peggy might have a form of what psychologists call Collier Brothers' syndrome, a unique condition where a person cannot throw anything away. Perhaps it strikes more people in poverty, when an individual does not know if he'll be able to afford another newspaper or a magazine, so he becomes much more likely to hang on to every single thing he can. Even the smallest possession, like a ten-year-old magazine or a three-year-old piece of mail, becomes incredibly significant. Still, I had no idea just how serious Peggy's situation was.

Digging In

George followed me back upstairs to the office while he waited for me to make a few phone calls. Thankfully, it was the summer, and we had a number of volunteers who were serving at Graffiti. I called an advocacy lawyer I knew and left a message for her about Peggy's situation. I was then able to reach a few members from the church who might also be able to meet at Peggy's apartment. George could hardly contain himself.

As we walked over to her apartment, my "priestly" friend lectured me on the venality of landlords in the Lower East Side. He was interrupted by the greetings of several people as they passed us on the street. "Hello, Father," or "Pray for me, Father," to which George nodded his head and kept talking with me without missing a beat. By the time we arrived at Peggy's building, I realized I would need to talk with her alone; George's remarkable ability to offend almost everyone he talked to probably wouldn't help us right now.

"George, you can't go in with me to talk to her. I'll have to catch up with you later. Why don't you check on the people in the squat across the street? They may need your assistance as a minister." George nodded again emphatically, pronounced his blessing on me, and strolled off to counsel his "parish." I buzzed Peggy's apartment.

"Go away!" Peggy shouted over the intercom when I buzzed her. "Leave me alone!"

"I just want to talk to you for a minute," I shouted into the metal box at the door. I waited. "Come on, Peggy. It's me, Taylor." Finally the buzzer on the door let me in, and I walked down the hallway to her apartment. Within seconds I began to smell the odor of cats and stale clothing. I knocked on her door, a ramshackle piece of wood with boards nailed on haphazardly, apparently to strengthen it. It rattled and creaked as she pulled the door open a few inches, staring at me through the crack. The smell of garbage hit me in the face.

"I've got to be careful!" she whispered. "The landlord's out to get me. Any time now." Her eyes grew wide with fear, looking more and more like Bette Davis's Baby Jane character. "The landlord says I've got to clean up my mess, but he just wants to get me out. He hates me. This crap about a clean-up is just a cover-up. He won't fix anything in my apartment. Come in! Come in!" she said suddenly. With ferocious irritation, she opened the door wider, pulled me in, and quickly slammed the wobbly boards shut.

"I can't tell you all this while you're standing in the hallway. He's got spies everywhere," she said, locking all three locks on the door. I glanced from her Bette Davis face to the room where she lived and instantly struggled both to find air and to keep my footing. I could barely believe my eyes.

In Peggy's entire apartment, there was only enough room for us to stand next to the door. She had managed to keep a space clear for the door to open, and there was a short path to an old mattress that slanted toward the ground at a ridiculous angle. Her apartment was large with high ceilings, but every single available space of it, except where we stood, was filled with clothing, newspapers, and paper bags.

The debris was not piled up just two or three feet high; rather, it rose ten to twelve feet high, from floor to ceiling. I saw walls of garbage stacked in gravity-defying pinnacles, streams of clothing, and shredded newspapers dangling precipitously from cliffs of debris. At the top of a cliff of clothing, an old tricycle or a shopping cart (I couldn't make out which) was jutting out of the mounds of material stacked at astonishing angles. I looked up to the ceiling in wonder. Peggy—dear Peggy—seemed completely unaware of the mountainous landscape around her.

"I think the landlord is trying to have me killed!" she hissed. "Someone was trying to get in my back window last night."

If there was a back window, I couldn't see it. I could make out on one side, in the small space between the wall of garbage and the ceiling, a faint glow of sunlight. I speculated that past the tons of gathered clothes and little paper bags there might be a window.

Peggy's eyes got even wider than before. "He'll use any excuse to get me out. He says my apartment is too cluttered. He doesn't have a leg to stand on. It's just an excuse," but then her voice broke. "Can you help me?"

"I don't know, Peggy. We're going to try. That's why George came to get me." In the little space next to the door, surrounded by an imposing landscape of litter, I told her that I still had a few more phone calls to make about her situation, but wondered if it would be all right with her if some friends came by to help. She nodded her head nervously, eyes darting from pile to pile. Then Peggy—frail and angry as she was—let me say a prayer for her. To myself I thought again about Bette Davis: *Here's what happened to Baby Jane!*

I returned to the office in time to answer the call from the Legal Aid lawyer. She was sincerely concerned for Peggy's situation, troubled by a system that too often disregarded the real needs of the poor or mentally ill. I had known this lawyer from other situations where friends were getting evicted, appreciated her advocacy work, and trusted her wisdom. In fact, I was relieved to hear her voice. No one could do this kind of work alone.

"Peggy will get a seventy-two-hour eviction notice any day now, Pastor. The landlord says her apartment is a health hazard to every tenant in the building, and of course he's right. Collier Brothers' syndrome," the lawyer's words marched on like a drumbeat. She spoke with conviction and determination. "We can't wait around," she went on. "Let's just rent a dumpster and clean the place out. We can do it in a day. She'll fight it, but if we don't do something, she'll be homeless and on the street in a week." I told her about my visit with Peggy and that I'd already found a few folks to help. I knew Bill would be willing to help; he always was. So were some of our volunteer summer interns and a few other Bible study faithfuls. We agreed to meet at Peggy's the next day.

By the time we arrived at Peggy's, the lawyer from Legal Aid was already there in front of the apartment, arguing furiously with Peggy.

"We can't do it today," Peggy shouted, eyes scared and anxious. "I don't feel well today. You'll have to wait until another day."

"No way!" said the lawyer. "This is the day we're moving this stuff out." When she saw me coming with the others, she got more stern with Peggy.

"See, your pastor's here and other friends. Now, let's get started." Begrudgingly, Peggy opened the door, and for the next several hours, ten of us carefully placed what seemed like Peggy's entire life in black plastic trash bags. Some pulled bags from the sides of the cliffs next to the door. Garbage high up began to teeter. Small avalanches occurred. Other people scrambled up with me to the cramped space between the garbage and the ceiling. We lay on our bellies and began to roll garbage down the slopes toward the door.

"Don't take that," Peggy yelled. "That coat is valuable! You can't take those, either," she said as she pointed to some old bottles and cans. "I can trade those in. I haven't read those newspapers yet," she blurted out as she pointed to some yellow, soiled papers. "You just can't throw those out!"

But we had to throw them out or Peggy would lose her home. We continued to work and negotiate every armload of garbage. We knew we had to do it, but to be honest, it felt like a robbery. We were taking away the possessions that had given our friend Peggy even the slightest ounce of significance.

As we continued, we found it most effective to work from the top down. "Is this what you were trained to do in seminary?" Bill was hollering to me with a smirk on his face as we threw stuff down. "You're not that good at it," he grinned, and I laughed at his question. I also couldn't help wondering what my brother, Robin, would have thought of this. Still, I found it interesting that this woman—like so many of us— also found whatever meaning she had in her life through what she owned.

Eventually, we were able to dig down to the top of Peggy's wardrobe closet, then the top of her refrigerator, then the stove. Like archaeologists, we dated the levels of debris from newspapers and artifacts. When Bill cut himself on a piece of glass, he asked, "Can you get AIDS from a piece of glass?"

"I don't think you can here," I said as I kept working and reading. "Look at this newspaper. We're down to 1977. I don't think AIDS was around then."

Bill crawled away into another room to get a Band-Aid. He came back a few minutes later to tell me the others had found Peggy's pet cat. "From magazines in the layer of trash, they figure the cat died about twelve years ago," he said flippantly, as if all was normal. I stared at him. Then I swallowed and closed my eyes for a second.

"Hey, I thought you were supposed to be a priest or something. Are you sure this is what you're supposed to be doing with your time?" he teased again.

"Nope, I'm not sure, Bill," I said, and rolled a bag of tin cans from the 1970s to Ron, a college student from Texas who was helping us that summer. We kept working. Finally, we uncovered Peggy's kitchen sink, her bed, her toilet, a couple of chairs, and a desk. Ron even got the toilet working again, which was no small thing considering the fog of dust so thick we could barely see in front of us. We looked like commandos, smeared with dirt, blending into our environment.

And all the while, Peggy stood—Bette-Davis-like—cursing at us for what we were doing to her valuables, for how we were disrupting her life, shouting at each of us that we were killing her. Part of me had to admit she was right.

When the apartment was relatively empty some eight hours later, Peggy accused the lawyer and me of working with the landlord to steal her valuables. But to Ron, she reached out her hand to shake his. "Thank you," she whispered and walked out to further chastise the lawyer. Ron came up to me and took me aside. "Pastor, she just gave this to me," he whispered, holding up a hundred-dollar bill. "I can't take this. She's a bag lady. She's got nothing. I can't *possibly* take this."

"Don't you dare give that back to her," I whispered back. "Do whatever you want with it, but don't you dare give that back to her. That is holy money. Go thank her, and put it in your pocket."

When I got home, Susan made me go outside because I smelled so bad from Peggy's apartment. As I removed what clothes I could out in the hallway, I thought about the lesson I learned that day about values and treasures: Even in her crisis, when it looked as if her dignity was being completely stripped, this "bag lady" with virtually nothing to her name but a small apartment on the Lower East Side, reached into her pocket and gave a college student a hundred bucks. My mind returned to the conversation I'd had earlier that week with my brother, and I was startled again at God's amazing ability to turn upside down the values and perceptions we bring to each situation. And though Peggy stayed mad at me for awhile, she was at least able to stay in her apartment.

The next Wednesday night, Peggy came to Graffiti for dinner and Bible study as usual. She came again the next week and the next. We'd found a treasure indeed.

The "'Vival"

Not only did I learn that my visiting church prospects was different, I also learned that our "church events" were going to be different too. Our little church began to grow, and we were casting around for our own way to include others. "When I was growing up, we had revivals," I explained to Bill, our music director. Bill had grown up in Brooklyn and now lived in a squat (an abandoned building). He looked at me as if I were speaking another language. "A revival," I continued, "is where you give yourself to the Lord or rededicate yourself to the Lord. It's a time for the church to get renewed or revived. But Graffiti wants to have a 'vival. You can't get *re*-vived until you've gotten *vived*."

"I'm in," Bill said, somewhat unenthusiastically.

"Let's see now," I said. "We need someone to be in charge of publicity. What about Don? I know that he just sat on the outskirts of the Bible study for six months, but now he has accepted the Lord and taken a stand. He has all that experience with pornography and the theater. He'd be wonderful in helping communicate. Then there's Clara. She may curse during the Lord's Supper, but she likes people. She used to live in Central Park and knows how to get along with all kinds of people. She could be in charge of visitation. Then there's Joey, who used to be a crackhead standing on the corner of Sixth Street. That was just a few months ago, but he's doing so much better now. He knows how to talk to people too. He'd be great at getting some ushers and greeters." I was beginning to get worked up. Bill was politely enduring me. "We'll need a bigger space too. We can't fit everyone into the storefront. What about the abandoned high school two blocks away? Maybe the group homesteading there will give us some space."

The group that was homesteading the old high school wasn't exactly enthusiastic about our meeting either. The idea of a church-type group doing something in their space provoked some strong feelings about institutional religion.

Once they reluctantly agreed to rent us some space, they showed me into an old room in the back of the high school. It was dark and dirty and had some folding chairs in it. I couldn't figure out what it had been originally, but it had been transformed into a place for parties. Almost everything was painted black. A long, homemade bar extended along one entire side of the room.

"What a great place for a 'vival!" I said.

Now came the preparation. Don, the ex-pornographer, got the publicity materials. One of the things he received from denominational headquarters was a box of lapel pins with a revival message on them: "Here's Life!" Don had a great hat and hair down to his waist, but no lapels. He put the pins in the holes in his ears. "That looks really good!" we all told him.

We went to a revival preparation seminar held uptown. The man who led the seminar was from Nashville. Our group, with its layers of clothes and smell of burning wood, didn't quite fit into the rest of the conference. At one point, the leader said, "The key to revival is door-to-door visitation."

George, who was still wearing his priest's collar and still had not received his mail-order ordination papers, got up. He'd probably had more experiences living in an abandoned building than anyone else in the group and shouted with gusto, "That didn't work for me! I tried door-to-door visitation in my building, and they burned my door down!" The seminar leader fiddled with his tie and tried to continue with his presentation.

After the seminar, we got organized. We cleaned up the party room at the old high school. We got a speaker. The day to begin finally arrived. People began to trickle in. Joey, the former crackhead, had gotten a wonderful group of ushers who were greeting people with high fives and then sauntering down the aisle with them to be seated.

"Oh, no," I told Bill, our music director. "Here comes Big Jane." Big Jane liked to hang with the squatter anarchists, and she hated Christians. She used to shout at us as she walked by the place where we handed out sandwiches. She called Christians and social workers "Poverty Pimps." She especially disliked Christians who came to the park where the homeless people were, handed out gospel tracts, and then went home. "Christoids," she called them. She had brought her dog with her to the 'vival . . . a little fluffy mutt with a rope as a leash. "She's going to disrupt our whole meeting," I told Bill. Big Jane sat in the back with her dog and looked around suspiciously.

Jim had left his dog at home but carried a hammer in his belt. He eyed the bar along the side. "When will drinks be served?" he shouted as we started to sing. Our voices sounded feeble and weak to begin with in that dark hall, but as we sang, we began to warm up.

The preacher, Dr. Ken Lyle, knew our neighborhood, and even though there was a little heckling at the beginning, people started listening to what he was saying. He talked about how Christ helped us to become who we really are. As we sat there between the bar and the black walls, we began to sense God's presence. "You don't have to be a big shot to know God loves you," Dr. Lyle said. "And you don't have to be like someone else. A friend of mine is named Willie. One day, Willie shared in our prayer group that his nine-year-old nephew had a terrible disease and was going to die. It was a very hard time."

Our group of people (and the dog) got very quiet. "On the day of his nephew's funeral, Willie came to our prayer group after the service. We all prayed for him. As we were praying, Willie began to laugh. Afterward, he explained that he was remembering the last time he had talked to his little nephew.

"Willie and the father of the little boy were sitting in the living room. The little boy was weak, but he asked his dad, 'Dad, do I have to wear a suit at the funeral?'

"His dad knew how he hated suits. 'No, son, I don't guess you have to wear a suit.'

"'Can I wear my favorite T-shirt?' the little boy asked.

"'Why, yes, son, I suppose you can.'

"And that was the way the little boy was buried—in his tennis shoes and blue jeans. His favorite T-shirt covered his emaciated body. Written on the front of his T-shirt were these words: 'I'm Glad I'm Me.' Let's pray together."

Very simply, the preacher explained what it meant to turn away from your sins and to let Jesus be the Lord of your life. He explained how Christ comes to you where you are and lives "in you as you" to be all you were meant to be. Bill led us in a song, and people were invited to come forward to the front. Everyone fumbled with their song sheets and began to sing. No one came forward. We continued to sing, and planned to close out the music. Out of the darkness at the back of the room Big Jane emerged, wearing her oversized overcoat. She began to walk slowly down the aisle. My first thought was that she was going to come forward to shout at us. She brought her little dog on a leash with her. There was a column in the aisle, and she walked on one side and the dog walked on the other. The little dog's eyes bulged, and it made a gagging noise before it found a way to follow Jane. Big Jane bowed her head and said she wanted to ask Christ into her life. Jim, with the hammer in his belt, came down to stand by her and committed his life to Christ too.

After the service, George with his collar, Don with the lapel pins in his ears, Clara who used to live in Central Park, and Peggy who looked like Bette Davis, crowded around Big Jane and Jim. We hugged them and laughed nervously, we were so happy. Don grinned and said to Big Jane, "Could you help me tomorrow night? I'm in charge of publicity, and I think you have some talent. . . ." We had gotten 'vived.

chapter five
Slow Deaths, Fast Lives

After Peggy's treasure hunt and our 'vival, I began to notice regularly just how fragile life seemed. Every time I turned a corner or answered a phone call or led a Bible study, someone was on the brink of crisis. I had always known in my head that urban living could take its toll on people, but when good friends began confronting death in knife fights, muggings, or illnesses, the reality of sad, painful living began hitting home. And when one friend got so drunk one night that he fell asleep on a heater, wound up in the hospital, and died days later of third-degree burns, the heaviness of despair started to weigh on me. I realized that on the Lower East Side (as in many low-income urban areas) death can be an everyday event. Whether it's the death of a dream, a relationship, a job, or a life, I suppose most urban pastors feel as if they are working in a war zone, battling constant emergencies. Death and dying become as common in their pastoral routines as Sunday school and Communion.

Still, this "life or death" mentality could get a little out of perspective. When I was working, for instance, in San Francisco at a Franciscan community service program, one administrative nun used to tell me, "Taylor, there are no emergencies but blood or fire." In other words, she seemed to understand that unless she set some firm boundaries, her life would be full of the type of interruptions that really could wait. Yes, the daily drama of urban ministry often meant someone had just pulled a gun on someone else or a neighbor was getting evicted. But it also meant—as I was beginning to see—that, well, what was a crisis to some urban folks didn't have quite the same value to others. The truth is that in most cities, the highs are higher and the lows are lower and the space in between is smaller.

So after a few hard lessons, I began to realize the accuracy of the nun's maxim: the only real emergencies were either blood or fire. Nothing else was really worth dropping everything for or worth losing my peace of mind over. In fact, I learned that even blood was not always an emergency. A man would receive a huge gash in a fight in the park, but he would then wait eight hours for medical care at Bellevue Hospital. I began to look forward to the day when the victories outnumbered the defeats, wondering, hoping they were just around the corner.

My First Funeral

In the meantime, though, I still had to confront the effects of death on a regular basis. One cold day in December, an older member of our Bible study, Jacob, came to me, weeping. Great tears dribbled from his cloudy gray eyes. His bottom lip turned down as he sobbed, shaking the white whiskers on his chin. It wasn't unusual for Jacob to come talk with me. He would sit in the back of our Bible study in order to keep warm on cold nights and stay longer than the others just to chat. One time, he wanted to talk with me about trees in the Bible.

"In a sense, every tree is a tree of life," he exclaimed like an old Hebrew prophet, his white beard and noble profile exclaiming each point. "When I'm in the park, I look up at the big trees that have been there so long, and I feel good as I watch the branches and the leaves wave in the wind. It reminds me of when I was a little boy and I would climb the trees. I felt so safe when I was sitting up there." Then he proceeded to tell me the various types of trees he thought were scattered throughout the Old Testament. I sipped my coffee and listened. I noticed his shoes were mashed down, and he had the same socks on his feet as he had the week before. I handed him a new pair of socks and watched him change them as he kept telling me about trees. His toes were dark with frostbite.

Jacob was a little different from some of the other homeless friends we'd met. He never used drugs and was very concerned about what he ate. I had never seen him argue or become violent with anyone. Basically, Jacob was always homeless in our neighborhood for one simple reason: he had eight large, mangy black dogs.

All the dogs looked alike to me, but Jacob could call each by name. When he'd walk down the street, all of them tied together in a tangle of ropes, he looked like an inner-city Santa Claus calling his reindeer: "Get over here, Blackie! Stop that, Shortie! Don't you bite him, Soapie!" They'd move as one organism, one blob of dark fur and rope, sending anyone walking by to the edge of the sidewalk.

"Oh, I love my dogs," Jacob would tell me in Bible study, closing his eyes dreamily. I could hear the dogs barking and yipping tied to a pole outside. "They're my children. You know that old squat on Sixth Street? I used to live there, but they threw me out. They said eight dogs was too many. They said I'd have to get rid of a few. Can you imagine that? What do they think I am? Would *you* get rid of a few of your children in order to stay in an apartment? Do you think that's right? My dogs are so sweet." I could hear them outside, growling and snapping at someone trying to step by, a loud short curse in response. "When I'm cold at night, they all cuddle up around me and I feel so warm." He looked up at the ceiling and smiled broadly, looking less like a Hebrew prophet and more like St. Nick.

But he wasn't smiling as we stood on the sidewalk on that cold day in December. Considering all of our conversations, this was the first time I had seen my homeless Jewish friend cry. Then I found out why.

"Pastor, Blackie has died," he paused for a second, looking toward the street. My mind raced over the faces of men at our Bible study, but I couldn't remember anyone named Blackie. Jacob continued.

"I don't know what to do. He was my *favorite*. He was so precious. I had him longer than any dog. I don't know what to do. I can hardly move. Will you help me? Will you help me bury Blackie?"

Jacob's eyes were red, and tears spilled over as he inched closer to me for help. Now I understood why Jacob was so upset. In a sense, a member of his family had died, and he was grieving his loss. Unfortunately, my schedule was completely full that day.

"Here, Jacob," I said, putting my hand on his shoulder. "Of course I'll help you. I'll call the American Society for the Prevention of Cruelty to Animals (ASPCA), and they'll help you take care of Blackie."

Horror filled his face and he took a step back from me, as if I had uttered a blasphemy or a threat he could not live with. "Never!" he proclaimed. "I could never take Blackie to the ASPCA. They treat dogs like, like . . . *animals.*" His eyes flinched in pain; his head shot back and forth in firm agony.

I tried to reason with him. "Jacob, they do this all the time," I said quietly, hopefully, thinking of my meetings. "They help people with their dogs. That's what they do."

But Jacob would not hear me, and he began to walk down the street. "Then I'll get someone else to help me," he called over his shoulder.

For a few heavy seconds, I watched Jacob the Hebrew prophet, the St. Nick of the Lower East Side, the grieving homeless man whose dog had just died, walk sadly into the busy city. I sighed a silent prayer. This *was* a crisis to Jacob. Then I heard myself calling after him.

"Wait a minute; wait a minute," I shouted, hurrying to catch up with him. "What do you want me to do?"

Jacob stopped instantly and turned toward me.

"Please just come help me bury him," he was weeping again. "I want to bury him next to my tent on the vacant lot on Eighth Street. Please help me."

It was a dark gray sky, getting grayer and darker. I pulled my warm coat around me, nodded in acceptance, walked to the church to get a shovel, and went with Jacob to the lot on Eighth Street. His house was a collection of boxes and blankets and plastic sheets on a littered, empty lot. There were other tents scattered around the lot, a sad commentary on the housing situation in New York. Jacob hadn't even been able to find a squatter building that would let him stay with his dogs, much less an apartment. Ropes, plastic, and string had become his makeshift home.

The dogs were tied up and howling. Pete, a tall African American man with high cheekbones and deep-set eyes, joined us. Pete and Jacob watched out for each other, and I had often seen the two playing chess in Tompkins Square Park. When Pete saw us coming with the shovel, he motioned us over to a spot he had claimed as Blackie's grave.

It seemed to be getting colder and grayer by the minute. Though the ground was rock hard, we began to dig. Slowly, we leveraged out big chunks of brick and broken glass. Pete and I worked at a snail's pace, half-inch by half-inch, trading off with the shovel and grunting in the awkward silence. Jacob was sitting on a bucket turned upside down, wailing.

About a foot and a half deep, we hit cement. "There must be a slab of concrete under this lot," Pete announced. While we stood panting over our failed attempt at digging a grave, a woman arrived. She had dirty hair, wore three overcoats, and her eyes were wild. "She used to help feed the dogs," Pete whispered to me, pointing.

"It's all your fault that Blackie died"—the woman hurled the words at Jacob—"You never took care of him. It's all your fault! You're a *bad* man!"

Jacob put his face in his hands and began to moan. Tension was rising in the woman as she shouted louder at Jacob. Pete and I tried to determine what we should do next. We knew Jacob would never agree to go to the ASPCA, but we also knew the hole we'd dug wasn't deep enough to bury the dog. Pete suggested we take the dog to the river. By this time, Jacob was walking around the tent shouting and wailing with the woman following him, screaming ever louder.

I shook my head, suddenly aware of how strange this situation was, wondering how I had come to be here, frozen by both the winter chill and my indecision. I tried to find something from my past experience to help direct our next step. There was nothing.

Pete, sensing my confusion, went to the tent where Blackie lay. Several rats scurried out from under the blankets as Jacob's tall friend dragged the dead dog from the tent. Jacob and the woman jerked to a halt when they saw the pet's stiff body. It was huge and looked more like an Angus cow to me than a dog. I held out a black plastic bag, and with great effort Pete slid the dog in. Together, we hoisted the bag and dropped it in an old shopping cart.

We started rolling the cart in a creaking funeral procession toward the East River. Jacob followed about twenty yards behind us, his head down, his white beard swaying in the December cold. The woman stood at the tent and screamed, her voice fading the closer we got to the river.

"Have you ever done a funeral?" Pete asked.

"Not in New York," I said.

I kept thinking of a woman from the neighborhood who had volunteered with us briefly in our Sunday school at the mission. One day, several months after she stopped working with us, someone brought us an old newspaper clipping about this same woman. Apparently, long ago, she and her lover had taken their dead baby to the East River and dropped it in. Later, she served time in jail for some drug-related crimes. Now, as we rolled

Blackie to the river, I felt somehow like a criminal. It felt like we were also doing something shameful. Yet, there did not seem to be any other options.

When we got to the edge of the river, we found some bricks, placed them in the bag and tied it up. Our bearded Hebrew prophet was absolutely quiet now.

"OK, Pastor," Pete instructed me. "Say some words."

I stood by the cart and took off my stocking cap. It was twilight and cold, and no one else was around. I swallowed hard. No seminary training had prepared me for this.

"Um, well, we are gathered here to remember Blackie. He was a good dog. Blackie was a good friend to Jacob." Jacob nodded his head and looked at the ground. "He kept Jacob warm on many a cold night. We know that God loved Blackie." I paused as we looked toward the water. I shifted my weight to keep warm. Pete did too. Jacob did not move.

"Now, I guess we should pray," I announced as we dropped our heads and closed our eyes. "Dear Lord, we yield this precious creature back to you. Thank you for the gift of life. Amen."

Pete picked up the stiff carcass in the bag and balanced it for a moment on the railing of the river. Then with a strong shove, we pushed the body over the side into the river. It landed with a lonely splash. Instead of dropping to the bottom of the river, though, the dog floated downstream because of the air in the bag. In pathetic silence, we watched the bag flow with the water's current.

"Just like a Viking," Pete murmured. I glanced at Jacob, whose face had the frightened look of a father who had just buried his child. Then he nodded at me. I shivered in the December air. I had almost missed this opportunity with Jacob.

Life Turns

Not long after Blackie's funeral, I arrived at the church office one morning to find a message from Bill scribbled on our message board: "Jacob is worried that they will close the lot on Tuesday!" I picked up the phone and made some inquiries about the lot, but I never expected the city would close it quickly. I made a mental note to check on Jacob next Tuesday, and then got on with the usual demands of my day.

After a weekend of relative calm, a blizzard of snow awaited us on the streets Tuesday morning, wind blowing so hard I could hardly see my way toward the church. I assumed we had a reprieve from any city action on that day. While we were giving out sweaters, socks, and gloves at Graffiti's clothes closet that morning, I heard rumors that something had happened to the lot on Eighth Street. A neighbor told me how the police would sometimes choose the worst day of the year in terms of weather to "clean up the neighborhood" because that way they would receive the least amount of public response and publicity. I wrestled with the words. Surely, they wouldn't do anything in this kind of weather. Then I heard more bad news.

"They shot at Jacob's dogs and took Jacob to Bellevue in handcuffs," someone said. Immediately I dropped the clothing I'd been handing out, grabbed my coat, and worked my way through the snow to the lot where Jacob and Pete lived. By the time I arrived, however, a bulldozer had already leveled the fifteen or so cardboard and plastic structures that had been there. Jacob's little house was gone, and no trace was left of our St. Nick or his dogs. I felt devastated and scared. I hurried back to the church and called the community affairs police officer.

"Yeah, I was there," he said indifferently. "Some of the old guy's dogs broke loose and bit a police officer. We didn't shoot any of them, although we had the right to. Instead, we 'darted' them, and now they're at the ASPCA. Jacob is at Bellevue Hospital, the psychiatric ward. I don't know why, but he was pretty upset."

I swallowed hard. A life had just been disrupted, a man's pets had just been taken from him, the only thing he knew as home had been razed, and this officer couldn't understand why Jacob was upset? The police officer's remarks reflected the kind of statements that used to make sense to me. Now they seemed crazy.

Then, as if to justify their actions, he made one final comment. "Incidentally, you should have seen all the rats that came out of his place when they bulldozed it. It was pathetic!"

I hung up the phone and walked back to the lot that Jacob and Pete and Blackie and Shortie and the other dogs had once known as home. I stared at the empty space, now collecting inches of snow across it. Suddenly, the woman with the dirty hair and wild eyes emerged from behind a trash bin and stood next to me in the quiet cold.

"This is nothing," she said as matter-of-factly as the officer had been. "Wait until they close the park."

I glanced at her wild face and watched as she walked into the blizzard. I tried to get Jacob out. Finally he was released from the hospital. Jacob was never quite the same after that; he'd faced crisis upon crisis, and it had begun to slow him down. Eventually he managed to find another lot, but never again did he talk much about trees or growing up or dogs.

On Easter of the following spring, a little group from Graffiti walked to the East River for a sunrise service. As the sun rose above the line of gray buildings, we sang a few Easter songs and thanked God for his gift of hope and new life in a world that often seemed chaotic or despairing. It had been a difficult spring, and we had lost several friends to death or drugs or the streets. We prayed together, ate bagels, and stood in the morning sun for a few moments of reflection.

When we finished, we looked out across the river, sunlight crossing the currents. It was a peaceful river that morning, and the only thing visible was a black dog swimming purposefully in our direction. At first, I thought nothing of it—that is, until my young son Owen shouted out, "Hey! It's Jacob's dog! He's resurrected!"

I smiled at the thought and wondered how the Hebrew prophet would feel hearing that. Maybe we were beginning to turn the corner after all.

New Living

As usual, the sun in the summer of that third year roasted each can of garbage on the sidewalk. The smells of urine, rancid vegetables, sticky ice cream, dog feces, and thrown-out flowers were trapped on the baking streets. Greedy flies buzzed around the receptacles. Most of the plastic trash cans had holes the size of softballs at the base where rats had eaten through, and bits of plastic trash bags or old food cartons were pulled partially out of these holes, evidence of the rats' work the night before.

The incredible July heat, mixed with an unusual amount of humidity, made even the smallest effort—like moving your bones—a monumental chore. Forget about breezes or air conditioning. Folks on the Lower East Side had long ago learned to live with excruciatingly hot summer weather, just as they did freezing blizzards in winter months. They gathered around the trees in the park, which provided a space a few degrees cooler than the baking streets, smothered in smog. Regardless, people were still struggling to make ends meet, still hungry for a decent meal; so in spite of the blazing temperatures, we decided to stick to our weekly schedule of ministry. We placed dozens of bags of sandwiches on a metal folding table on the hot sidewalk next to the park. Older ladies from Eastern Europe, young African American men, older Puerto Rican men, middle-aged Hispanic women with their children, Polish men, and heavy-drinking Caucasian punk rockers all began to gather listlessly in a line.

Everyone was cranky from the stifling weather. Angry homeless men began to crowd around the table, not wanting to wait long for a sandwich. Watching them, I recalled what a friend in San Francisco used to tell me: "I don't want to get theoretical about Christianity or some philosophy. I want to see something tangible, something concrete, like a sandwich in the hand." He would then hold out his hand and look at me.

But today the men pushed closer to the table, holding out their hands and grumbling for their meals. Their impatience got so bad that finally, Paul, the coordinator of the sandwich line, had to announce, "Get back. Please. Everyone will get one, but you'll have to get back!"

Yet this was a group of men who solved conflicts with their fists most days. They knew what they wanted, and they did *not* want to be told to "get back." So they did what came naturally: they told Paul to shut up, and they pushed harder.

"Now look!" Paul walked right up to the first one in line, a tall man wearing an old shirt, suspenders, dirty pants, and a vicious sneer, who was still telling Paul to shut up.

"I said look," he shouted again. His short framed body looked ridiculous next to the tall man in the suspenders. "Now this is the line of the *Lord!* I want you guys to line up right now." Some people got in line. Others stood where they were and stared at the small man who was ordering them to cooperate. Finally, Paul used his last resort, the one thing that he knew would get their attention.

"If you don't get in line, I'm going to come over there and *pray* for you!" That did it; the men grumbled and shifted. They knew he was serious. He'd walk over, lay his hands on the shoulders of some unsuspecting man, and pray fervently for a blessing. None of them wanted *that.* So when they heard his threat, every one of them got in line, meek as children.

After Paul offered a prayer of thanks for the meal, we started handing out sandwiches. By this time we had almost two hundred people waiting. There was a little shoving, a little cursing, and a lot of sweating, but the line began to move more smoothly.

Soon I was interrupted from the sandwich line by Bill and one of our other volunteers. "Pastor, you better come talk to this man over here." I sighed at the thought of moving again in this heat, but I slipped a sandwich bag into the next hands in line, excused myself momentarily from my duties, and strolled over to meet a strong, stocky white man in his thirties.

"Arthur," the man stated, offering me his hand in a firm handshake. "My name is Arthur." Then all at once, he looked up at the sky with wet eyes and began to sob.

"Let's go sit on a park bench and talk in the shade," I offered.

Arthur nodded and followed me to a bench across the street from the sandwich line. When we sat down, he put his muscletoned arms on his knees and let the tears flow harder. I wiped the sweat from my forehead and waited beside the man I had just met.

"This has never happened to me before," he finally exclaimed between sobs. "I'm a machinist; I usually make good money. But I lost my job. I started drinking. I lost my family too—my wife, my kids. I lost my car, my house, everything." He paused to find even an ounce of dignity so he could go on. I glanced up at the motionless leaves in the tree, then back at the sorrow on this man's face. He continued: "For the last three days, I've been on the streets. But just now when I came through that line, that guy who gave me a sandwich actually said something nice to me. To tell you the truth, it was the first kind word I've heard in a long, long time, and I just started crying. I don't know what's happening to me." He buried his face in his big callused hands and kept sobbing.

I prayed a silent prayer, feeling empty and helpless and hot. Then Arthur pulled out a grubby little pocket New Testament from his back pocket. "I've been reading this every day because I've got no one to talk to. Someone gave me this tract too." He pulled a soiled piece of paper from the New Testament to show me. He handled the tiny book very gently, as if it were a small animal, something alive and tender. The print was almost rubbed off the paper on some pages of the Bible. "I've read this a lot of times. Do you think this stuff is true?"

I stared into the searching eyes of this new friend, realizing God had indeed heard my hot and desperate plea. I admitted to Arthur that I did think this stuff was true. He asked me another question, I responded again, and we continued to talk back and forth, sharing stories and questions on that park bench until the line across the street had dwindled to just a few short tempers. Finally, while people were still shouting and cursing each other in the background, Arthur and I bowed our heads. He clenched his eyes shut and prayed as hard as he could to ask Christ into his life, to give him new life. I wiped my forehead again, relieved at the mercy we had just encountered.

As a new Christian, Arthur hit the ground running. "I want to know everything, to do everything just right," he said to me the next week. He looked like he had swallowed a light bulb. As soon as he'd finish one question, he'd blurt out another. But then one caught me off guard: "Will you go with me to Detox? I need a place to get straightened up." I explained to him what he might be getting into. It didn't matter, he said; he knew what he had to do and he wanted my support. We walked the couple of blocks together over to the Detox, a place where a person can stay for three days when he stops drinking.

"When was the last time you had a drink?" the worker at the Detox center asked, peering over his half-moon glasses at the two of us.

"It's been a day and a half," Arthur answered proudly.

"Sorry, that's too long ago. You won't pass the breath test, so you can't stay here."

What did he just say? Arthur hadn't had a drink for almost two days, and this worker was telling him he needed to be drunk now to qualify for this help. I was stunned. I felt as though I was standing in a foreign land. Arthur seemed to know exactly what the man was talking about.

"But I tell you what," the man at the Detox continued, setting down his pencil and paper. "Just go out and have a drink. Come back and take the breath test. I've got one more bed left for tonight."

"No way." Arthur was adamant. "I'm not doing that." He marched out of the center and onto the street. It took me a good minute before I realized I was standing alone, staring at this worker's glasses. I was still stunned at what I had just witnessed.

When I finally got outside, Arthur was pacing and taking deep breaths.

"No problem," he said. "I have a friend who can get me a place at a flophouse at the Bowery Mission. No problem. When's your next Bible study? I'll see you then." He marched off toward the Bowery with firm resolve, and I staggered home like a soldier shot in battle.

For the next two weeks, Arthur attended every Bible study, worship service, outreach event, and fellowship group Graffiti offered. He listened intently. He marked up his Bible. He cleaned up the storefront, and he kept asking questions. He even told anyone who'd listen, every group who came, what the Lord had done for him. He loved telling people about the new life God had given him through Christ. I'd never seen anything quite like it.

After two weeks of unbroken zeal, though, Arthur disappeared. For someone who usually talked with me about everything, it was strange that he hadn't told me anything about leaving. He never even said good-bye. I looked for him at the Bowery Mission, but he wasn't there. It was as though he had vanished, and I wasn't sure I was ready to lose another friend that year.

Then one day I got a phone call from Arthur, along with news I had never expected to hear from him. "Pastor, I'm calling you from prison," he said, still sounding as upbeat as he had when he was with us. I cleared my throat and asked what had happened.

"That's the one thing I *didn't* tell you. When I met you, all the things I said were true, but I'd just escaped from prison. And I knew if I were a Christian, I'd have to give myself up. I escaped from a *minimum* security prison, but I'm calling now from a *maximum* security prison." He ended the call abruptly, something about a time limit the guard had given him, but Arthur promised to stay in touch. I hung up the phone, feeling stunned.

Arthur called again the following week, asking Graffiti to pray for the guy in the cell next to him. "He's just a kid, and he murdered his mom and his dad. He doesn't know anything, so I've been talking to him about what happened to me. Just pray for him!" I agreed to have the church pray for his "neighbor" and shook my head in awe at the way God was working in Arthur's life.

Several weeks went by before I heard again from Arthur. When I did, he gave me a report that the "young kid's accepted the Lord," and again we were asked to pray for him. I told him we would and asked Arthur to pray for our continued outreach at the park. He said he would.

By the fall, we were planning youth programs and discipleship classes for some of the friends who had come into a new Christian faith during our summer events. My schedule was still full and demanding, and each day I went from meetings to visits to Bible studies. Interruptions were happening less and less, and my heart continued to sing because of the ministry God had given Graffiti.

I'd almost forgotten about Arthur when the phone rang one busy afternoon just as I was leaving the office. Immediately I recognized the voice of the desperate—but changed—man I had met in the park that scorching July day.

"Guess what?" Before I had time to guess, Arthur continued in his usual excitement. "Another guy on our floor accepted the Lord. We're starting to have a Bible study together. Can you believe it?" I had to admit, I could barely believe it. But in the next six months, Arthur helped bring four more prison inmates into a relationship with Christ. He continued leading Bible studies, and he never stopped calling me and asking for prayer. When Arthur was finally released from prison, he decided to go back upstate and found a job in a Christian ministry there.

"You know how this all started?" he said when he called me from upstate to tell me what was happening.

"Was it when we sat on the park bench?" I asked.

"Nope."

"Was it from all the Bible study?"

"Nope."

"Was it when your friend accepted the Lord in prison?"

"Nope."

"Then when was it?"

"It was that peanut butter and jelly sandwich," Arthur said with earnest determination, "and the kind word that guy said to me in line."

All I could think to say in response was, "Is that right?" We hung up the phone, and I felt glad and humbled at the same time. I think that is when I finally realized that life and death situations on the Lower East Side are not always as they seem, that God loves to use small things.

Just how small, though, I was about to find out.

More Rats Than People
in New York City
—HEADLINE OF A DAILY NEWSPAPER

chapter
six
Of Rats and Men

Throughout those first couple of years in the neighborhood, we saw friends like Arthur and Jacob come and go, and I began to discover that urban ministry was much more transitional than I thought it would be when I first arrived. Whether it was getting evicted from an apartment or delivered from a drug addiction, finding a new job or changing an old belief, people's lives changed; and once they did, they often moved on. So not only had Graffiti Church become a small center of help on New York's Lower East Side, but it continued to be a revolving door for homeless friends, neighbors, and workers as well.

But there was one thing in our community that never changed. And for all the adjustments I had learned to make, all the good-byes and prayers and meals we had offered in the park, one segment of the population never moved on. Rats.

Rats depressed me. I never liked their attitude (I still don't) and was always bothered by their greedy persistence both in the streets and in the buildings where we lived and worked. I saw rats as good-for-nothing creatures whose only role in the natural order of life seemed to be to test our patience. One week in February, I became especially conscious of them as several rats fought and screeched along the wire fence behind our building. One particular rat the size of my hand liked to sit in a flowerpot we had hung from the fence post, and its casual indifference infuriated me. My wife had even put a pile of rocks on the back porch to throw at the rats in an effort to keep them away from our place. I told her that the gentle, Franciscan part of my soul could never do such a thing.

The learning curve, however, for urban living is great.

One evening I was sitting outside on the fire escape, thinking about the programs and events at Graffiti, musing over the areas in my life I needed to work on. The flowerpot-rat appeared, interrupting my contemplative moment and scurrying cockily along the walkway beyond our fence. I shouted at it, but it ignored me and continued its selfish search for food. Then without thinking, my hand grabbed a rock from the pile, pitched it like a baseball toward the fence, and watched it hit the fence just behind the ugly creature. The rat acted as if it had been electrocuted and ran for cover.

Another rat appeared. This time I was ready, and the rock landed directly underneath the rat's feet. Shocked by the unthinkable, the rat sprang for a hole in the debris.

Now I was consumed by the spirit of the hunt. I became the great rat scout, the rat hunter, with a rock in each hand. A huge rat, the granddaddy of rats, a corpulent, self-satisfied rat, appeared around the corner. I threw a large rock as hard as I could toward its arrogant face. The rock struck the ground in front of it, nicking its unsuspecting nose and turning its obese body in a total back-flip. It convulsed in surprise, and scampered back into hiding, licking the wounds of its pride. A fierce cry of triumph sprang from my chest and echoed down the dark corridor of the tenement buildings.

"I think I've found a new hobby," I told my brother on the phone the next day. He laughed as I explained about the alley rats. What I didn't know, however, was that this was just the beginning in my war with the rats.

Rats Rule

By the next summer, rats ruled. They were a symbol of all that was wrong in the neighborhood. They sauntered and screeched along the chain-link fence behind our building every night. They showed up in places where we never expected them. And they tore their way into the lives of friends or families in ways that regularly challenged my vision for what God could do through us.

An old man with stringy white hair, for instance, used to sweep up in front of our apartment building almost every afternoon. He always had a bottle in his pocket as he swept and was willing to greet you with a grizzled smile, even though he wouldn't say a word. He wore a dirty sandal on one foot because of a sore, and as the days passed, I watched with mild concern as the infection on the foot spread above his ankle.

When I didn't see him for several weeks, I asked a neighbor in our building what had happened to our sidewalk sweeper. I struggled to believe her answer: "That old guy? Oh, he died of a rat bite that got infected."

Another time Janie, a young mother of six, told me after church one hot Sunday how she had been in the emergency room the night before because a rat had bitten her baby, as if that were a normal part of their routine. Victor, the man with the rubber nose, overheard us and nodded his head emphatically, clearly understanding Janie's problem. The sixty-year-old Puerto Rican man loved wearing his sombrero and shouting, "Thank you, Jesus!" or "Santos, Santos!" at our church services. But when he heard Janie's story, his face became serious and he pointed to his eyebrow.

"A rat left a scar here on my baby," Victor told us, his finger tracing a vertical line over one eyebrow. Then he told us how all four of his children had also been bitten by rats in their childhood. I shook my head in disgust and wondered what we could do.

Monday morning I talked over the rat dilemma with one of my coworkers, Mary. Mary lived in an apartment above the storefront we used for some of our programs, and was the type of Christian worker who would stare down a sociopath without flinching. But when I brought up the rat issue, her face turned pale and fearful.

"Just yesterday my cat caught a baby rat in the bathroom. Something has to be done, Taylor," she said, her voice still shaking. Now *I* was afraid. Since first coming to Graffiti, I was learning to deal with people's pains or alcoholism or homelessness or various other crises, but I didn't know anything about rats. And I doubted our little rock pile would matter now.

That night, I managed to set two traps for the rats that had been invading our storefront for some time, putting a little dab of peanut butter on a plastic fork and placing it carefully on the edge of the traps without getting my fingers snapped. Then I set another trap and dropped an old slice of apple on the bait tray. Suddenly the trap snapped with a ferocious bang and flipped over from its own force. The noise reverberated through the empty storefront, and I felt eerily alone.

I fixed the trap, slowly pulling back the powerful spring and resetting it. I gently put the two traps in their positions. Then I stopped for a moment and said a prayer to God in the presence of the traps. It felt a little silly, but I was desperate to see something done about these threatening rodents. This was my rat prayer:

> God, I don't like killing things.
> I do this with resolve and remorse.
> Amen.

The next day, one of the two traps had been sprung. A small rat, about six inches long with a tail about the same length, had been caught. The trap had flipped over as it was sprung.

When I turned the trap back over, I looked at the face of the rat and wondered if there was anything I was supposed to learn by encountering this wretched parallel community. My son and I had discovered from the encyclopedia how the Norway rat, the common city brown rat, lives in groups called packs or colonies, which often contain more than two hundred rats each. Apparently, members of the colony recognize each other by a specific scent, and they thrive because they are smart and adaptable. They learn from their mistakes. If they eat poison and it makes them sick, they won't eat it again. And they are not easily destroyed since they've been found on every continent, even Antarctica. Able to thrive in a variety of environments, Norway rats go wherever humans go. Maybe that's one reason we don't like them. They're adaptable like we are.

"This isn't the big one," Maria, our bread volunteer, was now standing beside me and interrupting my thoughts. I picked up the dead rat's body with a shovel and listened more intently to Maria. "There's a big mama one around here somewhere, Pastor. It's your responsibility. You've gotta stop them! They infested my building, and one was on my bed once. See, they like the smell of babies and will bite them. Kids are in here all the time! You gotta protect our children!"

"OK, OK, Maria," I said, trying to reassure her of our strategy as I dumped the rat into a plastic bag. I smiled at her again, though I had no idea how in the world we'd really get rid of the rats. I prayed the rat prayer again.

The next day, however, coffee creamer was strewn across the floor of the storefront. We pulled the refrigerator away from the wall in the kitchen because we had heard sounds behind it and discovered a hole about four inches in diameter where a rat had gnawed through the baseboards and gained access to our kitchen. The thick plastic at the base of the trash can had a similar size hole. We felt like doctors searching for a cure for cancer. *That took planning,* I thought to myself, looking from the mess to the hole to the trash can. *That took tenacity, which is why these rats are so successful.*

When I asked a friend who knew something about construction how to seal the hole, I realized how much I still had to learn. I asked him if he thought a little wire net across the hole would seal it and keep the rats from coming in. He laughed at my idea.

"Wire? Huh! They're much too smart for that. You can be sure they'll find a way through flimsy wire."

So I did my best to board up the hole with thick plywood and nails, determined to get that "Moby Rat." But by the end of the week, Mary called me at home to tell me the rats had now gotten into the bread—bread that had been donated for the people in the neighborhood. It had been placed in big bags up high on the table. The rats climbed up and chewed on almost every loaf. All the bread that was to be given out to people in need had to be thrown away. It must have been that big smart one.

On Saturday, Bill helped me set another trap, and I said my rat prayer with more seriousness. This was getting to be too much. Our workers were afraid, and our resources were at risk. We also had to think about the filth and potential disease these disgusting creatures were spreading. I knew something had to be done, and I felt desperate for God to intervene. I set another trap—this one was big enough to break my finger. Like a surgeon, I carefully placed the peanut butter on the bait tray and stood up slowly. It had been a very long week; my neck was tight, and my eyes burned. I locked the door and stood alone in the storefront for a moment staring at the trap.

For some reason, my mind suddenly jumped to the Gospel of John where Jesus referred to the Hebrew account of the people of Israel wandering through the wilderness with Moses. They began to complain against God, and consequently were attacked by a plague of fiery serpents who bit the people so that many died. Standing in our storefront that day, I suddenly understood such horror, the scores of greedy snakes slithering into tents, biting babies, children, adults, the elderly. Wherever a person stepped or ate or slept, there was fear and horror.

Then I thought how strange God's solution was: he instructed Moses to fashion a three-dimensional picture and set it on a pole so that the people could look at it and be healed. What was the image? What did the people look at in order to live? God? The mercy seat? The ten commandments? An angel?

No. They had to look at the very object of their fear and loathing—the image of the snake (Num. 21:9). I then realized that Jesus chose this incident to describe what would happen to him on the cross (John 3:14–15), though the slow execution of the Son of Man would make us wince and want to turn away. Yet Jesus described his being lifted up on the cross as similar to the bronze snake being lifted on the pole; those who turned their faces toward him in his awful situation would live.

I turned to Jesus' face and walked home that night a little less concerned about the rat war.

By the next morning, as the storefront was as quiet and empty as a cathedral, I wondered what had happened to my trap. As I entered, I looked across the room and saw an enormous rat, ten or eleven inches long and completely still. It was the big mama, Moby Rat, and it was dead. The strong metal bar of the trap had caught the rat right beneath the head and without a drop of blood splattered on the floor, it was killed. Its fur was brown and healthy and sleek, and I looked straight at its face for a few seconds. Funny, I no longer felt afraid as I scooped it into a plastic bag and threw it in the trash.

Who Is the Enemy?

After I cleared things up, I went out to do some errands. Farther away from Seventh Street, the drug selling was less organized and more competitive. I was accosted by four or five drug dealers on each corner of First Avenue. Each one tried to look me in the eye and make their advertisement: "Cense, Cense, Smoke, Smoke." I scowled and walked faster, angry at what the drugs were doing to my friends and our neighborhood. What they did disgusted me. I was a little afraid of them too.

Then, for some reason, I felt compelled to slow down. I sensed the probing question: "Do you really love this neighborhood? Do you really love these people?" I slowed down further and tried to really look at these intense, aggressive young men who angered me so. One of them caught my eye, and when we made eye contact, he latched onto my arm like a leech.

"What do you want, man? I got good stuff, good stuff." To him, I was a nothing—one more suburban yuppie looking to score drugs in the inner city.

I slowed down a little more as he held onto my sleeve. "No thanks, friend. I have something better," I said.

"Something better?" his face screwed up in intense anger, sensing a deal. "Something better!" he shouted as I kept walking. He followed me halfway down the block. "There's nothing better than what I have," he said, holding up his cellophane bag of something. "Come on, show me," he shouted. "If you have something better than this, I'll give this to you. Now, come on," he said with a sneer. "What do you have that is better than this? You don't have nothin' better than this." He pointed to his bag.

"Oh, yes I do," I said, stopping and looking him full in the face. "Because what I have is real life in Jesus Christ." His angry face, about eight inches from my own, melted in shame.

"Oh, man," he said with a sigh. He looked down at the sidewalk in shame.

"You don't have to do this, friend," I said. "There's another way, you know."

He looked me in the eyes again and said, "Man, my father is a preacher." Maybe he told me that to show that he wasn't such a bad guy.

"Yes, but what about you," I said. We introduced ourselves, shook hands, and talked for a long time. He did not ask Christ into his life. He stayed with his buddies on the street corner as they hawked their goods. Yet after our conversation, he couldn't quite go back to selling either. After I had walked another block, I looked back at him, still standing there in indecision, a very miserable young man. On that day, my heart changed. I began to look at what frightened me, or disgusted me, more clearly. I saw that young man, not just as the enemy, but as part of my neighborhood too.

Reading the Signs

The months that followed the rat war made me wonder if rats weren't somewhat symbolic of the many things in the city we'd always have to fight against; maybe they were like the sins in our lives that would not go away on their own. We had to make conscious decisions how to deal with them. In a weird way, I learned to live with the rats and realized that, like most things, they required strategies to master them in the same way humans refine strategies to conquer their shortcomings.

One day Paul, our helper for the food line, was praying with someone in the park. Paul had lived a tough life, had once lived in New York's eerie underworld of abandoned subway tunnels (and could relate to rats), but had come up one day to encounter the face of Christ. Consequently, he had a tremendous burden for the people in our neighborhood and often did anything he could to help a friend meet Jesus. Usually that meant praying with them.

On this sunny Saturday afternoon in our food line, Paul was at work. He stood on the sidewalk with his hands on the shoulders of a young woman whose hair was dyed purple and whose nose was pierced with tiny gold rings, praying fervently that God would give this young woman a blessing. That was all. No

Engaged!

Our first apartment building

Taylor, Freeman, and Owen take a stroll

eeman, Susan, Owen, and
ylor in the park

Our boys in the 'hood

The family–all dressed up and nowhere to go

Squatter homes

Site of Jacob's home

Sleeping on the bench

Hard times in the Lower East Side

A "squat"–
an abandoned building

Tent city in the park

Getting warm in the park

Taylor shares Christ in the park

An inside look at life in a "squat"

Sharing a joke with a friend

City dreams

Help with clothing

A walk in the park

Wednesday prayer time

Taylor and a summer missionary

Volunteers pray before serving

A young Eli De Jesus and friends

Discussion after a Bible study

Graffiti Christmas card

Taylor soon after he arrived in New York

Susan works as a tuto

Eli De Jesus tutoring a student

li at his high school graduation

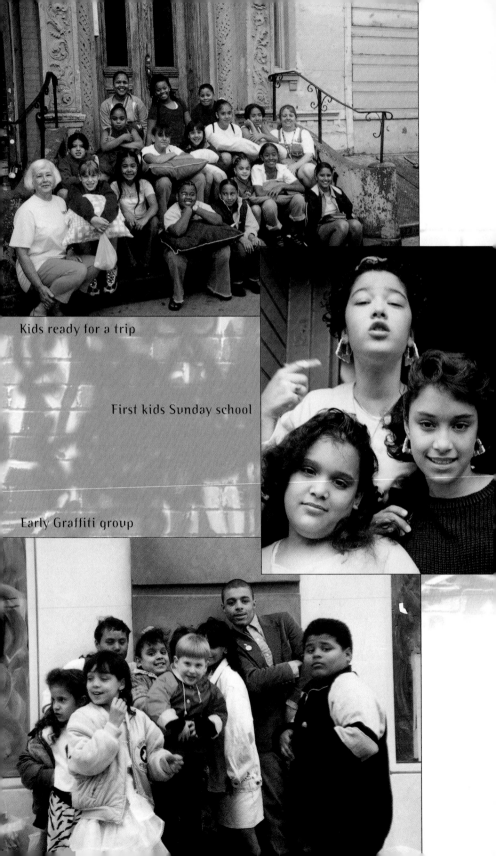

Kids ready for a trip

First kids Sunday school

Early Graffiti group

Graffiti gang on the front stoop

Changes in the neighborhood

theological or doctrinal discussions, no spiritual lectures or sermons, Paul simply offered a prayer that God would bless her.

An older woman, named LaGuardia, saw him praying with the purple-haired woman and, for whatever reason, walked over and meekly pulled on his sleeve.

"Will you pray for me too?" she muttered, barely loud enough for anyone to hear.

"Of course I will," Paul said, smiling at her. Paul turned his attention to the older woman and talked to her. He listened to her aching heart and told her how much the Lord loved her and wanted to free her from the trap she was in. She wanted forgiveness and agreed to ask Christ into her life. Then Paul placed his hands on her head, and did what he did best: he prayed. He whispered a gentle reminder of God's love for her, of Christ's sacrifice on the cross for her, and asked the Lord to give her a new life. Slow soft tears began to roll down LaGuardia's cheeks as she realized what was happening. Her life would never be the same.

For LaGuardia, it was a transforming moment on that hot summer day. (She confessed to Paul later that if he had told her to wait a minute, she would have run away.) Through Paul's prayer and her own commitment to follow Christ, LaGuardia instantly gave up a twenty-five-year drinking habit. After that, she smiled a lot and started coming regularly to Graffiti's services and Bible studies. She even brought her common-law husband, Mike, to the church the very next morning. This short Irish man with hair just like Ronald Reagan's got on his knees with Paul during Sunday school and asked Christ into his life too. Several other people in the Sunday school class who also understood some of Mike's story talked to him about what it meant to make Jesus the Lord of his life. It was all very new to him.

But Mike's conversion was not quite as radical as his wife's. He couldn't—or wouldn't—stop drinking. A few days after his church prayer, he ran up to me on Eighth Street one morning while I was talking with Bill about the abandoned building where he lived. Because Mike looked as though he had been hit in the face with a bag of rocks, Bill got the message that he needed to talk with me alone. My tall, black friend excused himself, and Mike jumped in.

"She threw me out, Pastor," Mike's wavy hair was turning furiously from side to side. "I can't believe it. She threw me out. What am I going to do now? She just threw me out, but I love her so much. I love her so much." When he stopped yelling, I got a whiff of where Mike might have come from. He reeked of beer. I took a step back, but he threw his arm over my shoulder.

"So what am I going to do? I know. I'll go to Detox. I'll go to the hospital right now. I'll do it." And with that, he marched toward the bus stop with determination, managing somehow to avoid colliding with anyone on the busy street. The next time I saw Mike, he was sober, calm, and in the hospital. We talked about his new faith and what choices he might need to make for the near future, knowing how difficult the battle would be to change his life. His jaw was set like a runner going up a steep hill, and though his hands shook a bit at the prospect before him, his voice was as tenacious as the last time I had seen him—and this time he was sober.

Once Mike was released from his Detox program, LaGuardia agreed to let him move back into their apartment. He jumped into the church activities with the same dogged determination with which he had jumped into drinking. He was at every meeting, Bible study, and outreach effort. He worked constantly to help us clean up and set up chairs and tables for our various gatherings. At each worship service, Mike sat on the edge of his seat, leaning forward and focusing as hard as he could on everything I taught in my sermons. He never missed a meeting at his recovery program and repeated to me everything he had learned. I was impressed with his efforts; others, too, were encouraged by his new commitment.

But it was not an easy war Mike had waged. Eventually, I began to notice that everywhere Mike went, LaGuardia was at his side. She was his eyes and ears. LaGuardia—who got her name because her mother first arrived from Puerto Rico at LaGuardia Airport—grew in her Christian walk almost effortlessly. She simply prayed in the park with Paul that day and was transformed. Mike, on the other hand, strained at every step, struggling to overcome his pride and independence. It was an amazing step forward when he announced in Bible study one night, "I'm Mike, and I'm an alcoholic," mirroring what he had learned at Alcoholics Anonymous. Then I watched him as we read the Bible together, noticing how he shifted in his seat next to LaGuardia.

"I need to get some glasses. I can't read this stuff," he'd muse, deflecting attention from his situation. Finally, after we'd gone through the Scripture lesson for the evening, there was a quiet moment. Mike jumped in: "You know what, everyone? I can't read at all. I just pretend to read, or I get LaGuardia to help me." He looked around the room with a scowl, daring anyone to laugh.

For once, no one said a word.

I thanked him for his honesty, and we ended the evening in prayer. Afterward, Mike and I made an appointment to go to an orientation for an adult reading program. When the day arrived, he talked nonstop as we walked to the subway together. Slowly, his troubled story began to unravel: Mike had been drunk so long he couldn't remember parts of this subway, though he was sure he had slept in it. He'd fallen asleep many days on a sidewalk or in a tunnel and would have to fight off the rats to protect whatever he'd scraped together for a meal. He'd beg on different corners, buy his beer wherever he could, and stagger through the park or the streets just trying to survive.

But that, he told me as we found a seat on the 6-train, wasn't as bad as prison. That was harder than anything, even harder than the times he had known as a boy growing up with an alcoholic and abusive father.

"My dad used to smack me all the time. He was a drunk," Mike proclaimed as the person beside us on the subway looked up from his newspaper. Mike continued: "He smacked me for little things and knocked me off my chair if I didn't put my fork down right. Or he'd hit me if I didn't wash a dish right. Finally, I ran away. That was better."

When our subway stop came, I began to see the city through Mike's eyes: the best places to beg, the safest places to sleep, the places to lie under when it rained. I realized that the subway was also filled with signs that gave important information Mike had never been able to understand. As we emerged from the subway exit onto the street, I studied the street signs, office buildings, and store names while Mike was taking other cues about where he was. Since this was not on his normal, memorized path, he was completely lost. He shadowed me like a child who was proud but terribly afraid. As we walked into the large building, I was aware of all the information given through signs. Mike stayed close to me, trying to act as if he were not confused.

While we sat quietly in the waiting room of the reading center, my mind wandered back to the time when seven teenage boys had accepted Christ at one time at Graffiti. What did our denomination usually do when someone accepted the Lord? We got them involved in Bible study and discipleship. I had gathered the seven teenagers in a circle and handed them each a Bible. Once I did, I quickly realized that five of the seven boys couldn't read at all. It became clear that poor, overwhelmed grade schools often dumped students into poor, overwhelmed middle schools that dumped the same students into poor, overwhelmed high schools. Very few graduated from high school in this neighborhood. As I glanced at Mike, I thought about the shame those boys must have felt in that Bible study. And I thought of what Mike's embarrassment must have been a thousand times a day as he improvised ever more clever ways to cover for himself. At that moment, my heart ached for Mike. I hurt for him; I admired his unsinkable effort to survive. I wanted to protect him.

Many other people were waiting in the center, as scared and excited as Mike was. Finally, an interviewer took Mike and me to a desk so that he could officially apply to the program. The interviewer was confident and efficient, looked only at Mike, and recorded all of Mike's answers on a piece of paper.

"This may seem hard right now," the interviewer told Mike, his eyes dark and kind. "But don't worry. You may not believe this, but I know exactly how you feel. You see, I was an adult who couldn't read either. I went through this same orientation a few years ago. I know how scary it is—don't be afraid."

I waited outside his office as Mike went through more interviews. The interviewer's gentle but firm manner with Mike touched me deeply. I thought about proud Mike. Mike who lived in subway tunnels. Mike who ran from cops. Little, determined Mike in prison. Mike who couldn't find the address to get help because he couldn't read the signs. Mike working hard to help at church. Mike hanging on to every word I preached at church, as if they were a doctor's instructions, the difference between life and death.

Suddenly, one of the interviewers came to me. "You'd better come see Mike. He's crying really hard." I was stunned. Mike never cried. He always had his jaw set and a serious scowl. Something must have really upset him, and I was sure he was going to quit before he started. Something must have made him mad. Mike's head was in his hands by the time I reached him, and he was wailing like a lost child who'd finally found his mother. "I can't believe it; I can't believe it," he blurted out over and over.

"You can't believe what, Mike?" I asked him, putting my hand on his shoulder, trying to comfort him. "You can't believe what?"

"I can't believe I really *am* somebody. I *am* somebody." That was the only explanation Mike would give me that day in the reading center. I settled into the chair beside him, smiled, and knew then that my friend had taken perhaps the bravest step yet in his battle.

Real Men

Over the next year, Mike slowly learned to read, and I watched how it changed each part of his life. He grew into an important friend in our church community, and I began to rely on him for many things.

"We're having a work team come next week to teach us some things," I announced one Wednesday night at Bible study.

"What's a work team?" Mike asked, clearing his throat at the same time and carefully closing the Bible on his lap.

"Good question." I looked over the faces in front of me and explained how a team from a large church would be coming to Graffiti to offer some practical help around the ministry and neighborhood. Since many of our members lived in a squat (an abandoned building), I explained how it might be helpful for them to sharpen their carpentry and electrical skills as well as learn some strategies to keep the building warm through the winter. The battle for survival on the streets required both thought and help.

"By the way, this is a team from North Carolina of carpenters and electricians and plumbers. Anyone interested?"

"I'll sign up. Hey, every little bit helps in the fight, right?" Mike volunteered, running his hands through his hair and looking at the others, expecting them to follow suit. Bill raised his hand to support Mike, and so did the others.

The following Saturday, a group of squatters and other interested people assembled in the storefront and waited for the workshop to begin. Larry had chains draped across the front of his coat and down the side of his legs. He wore a screwdriver through his ear. Jim, from the 'vival, had eight layers of clothing on, canopied by an old army jacket and held together with a wide belt. Through the belt was a big rusty hammer, which I knew Jim used for protection when he roamed the streets. Mildred sat in the corner, covered with a parka, resting her hand on a small cat carrier. The surly cat inside meowed defiantly. Shane had long blond hair held down with an old faded bandana and a mustache like General Custer's. May Day was another young man who sat in the corner wearing a fantastically torn and cut-up leather jacket. He would never look at anyone; his eyes darted quickly across faces and rooms. And then there was Mike, sitting patiently in the front row, sipping his coffee and talking with a few other friends who had come to the workshop. Bill helped serve coffee, smiling all the while at this strange collection of people.

The men from North Carolina looked like men from North Carolina. They wore colorful vinyl coats and clean baseball caps adorned with hardware insignias. Before we began, the leader of the group looked at the participants of the workshop, quieted down the crowd, and became philosophical about his first trip to our neighborhood. "You know," he said in a rhetorical voice, adjusting his baseball cap over his gray curly hair, "the people around here are so strange, that if you're not weird, you're odd." He chuckled at his own joke, but Larry, Jim, and Shane simply stared at him. Mildred clung to her cat cage. May Day's eyes shot up at the older Southern man, then around the room and back at the ground. No one said a word. *It could be a long day,* I thought to myself.

After a few awkward moments, the work team from North Carolina started pitching in, showing people some carpentry skills and explaining electrical principles. Shoulders shifted, voices muttered. Jim fingered his hammer in his belt and stood defensively as he watched the instructors. Mildred tried to act bored, as if she already knew everything the men were showing them. The surly cat sang its surly song.

By lunchtime, thankfully, people started warming up to each other. Jim stopped fingering his hammer and started telling any of the work team who would listen how wonderful his pit bull dogs were. "I love the dogs I have now. They wouldn't hurt a fly," Jim said as a few men grunted in response. Jim continued, "I had a beautiful dog last year. Sheba—she was beautiful. So beautiful that a drug dealer on Sixth Street wanted to buy her. I said no way, 'cause she was like my own daughter. He kept asking me, and I kept sayin' 'No way!' One day he got so mad at me, he took a gun out and shot her right there on the street in front of me." He looked down at his hammer; the men moved their boots uncomfortably from side to side. "I really loved that dog," he said.

Then during our lunch break, I overheard Shane as he "expounded" on his spiritual journey with one of the construction workers. "I was only a kid when they first came to me. They came through my wall at home—the three dark lords. They said they had a special mission for my life. I am on my way to fulfill that mission. Sometimes I must offer cats and dogs," he said with a strange grin.

"Man, you are out to lunch," the North Carolina construction worker said, unimpressed by Shane's story. "Don't you know there is another way? You need Jesus." Shane seemed a little disappointed, then simply smiled a knowing smile and continued to eat his soup. I offered a silent prayer for mercy.

By the afternoon, people were looking each other in the eye and beginning to laugh together. They went out in teams to the squats and apartments to put in insulation, fix windows, and put up Sheetrock, strategizing the whole time about how they might keep their places sturdy and strong year-round. They even plugged up some rat holes in our building. By dinnertime, many bridges had been crossed, walls had been built, and lives were made a little easier. I felt grateful for the successful exchange.

The next day we decided to hold a graduation ceremony and presented each participant with a diploma for their work. It was like no graduation I had ever seen before. Shane was roaring like a general, and Jim—with the eight layers of clothing—was whistling as if he were at a baseball game. Mike was patting everyone on the back for their good work, and Bill was singing with all his heart to back up the accolades. Wisecracks and jokes flew around the room like they do at family reunions. When a participant's name was called to receive his diploma, he strutted up to the front like a peacock, soaking up all the attention and applause he could get. Everyone laughed and almost everyone hugged. Mike then invited the North Carolina work team to join us the next day for church. They even agreed—albeit reluctantly—to sing a special hymn for us during the offering.

Worship services at Graffiti Church were not exactly what the men from North Carolina were used to. They did at least see many of the same friends who had attended the workshop, shuffling into the service, muttering or laughing or still strutting from yesterday's accomplishment. When we began the service, Paul led us in prayer, Bill helped us sing some hymns, and we all made room for some of the folks who always managed to stagger in late. When it came time for the offering, though, no one could have prepared us for what would happen next.

The work team dutifully walked to the front, opened their hymnals, and began to sing. They were nervous, but they held their notes. Mildred was responsible for passing the offering bag this Sunday, and somehow she'd made the decision that just because the team was singing, it was no excuse for them not to give. She walked right up to the first man in the line and stood reverently next to him, tapping him gently with the offering bag. Then she waited for him to make an offering while the tall, red-faced man tried to follow in his hymnal.

I tried to catch Mildred's attention. "Pssssst! Mildred!" I shook my head and pointed to the offering bag.

Either she didn't see me or she didn't want to. She tapped her foot as she waited for him to contribute. The construction worker finally reached in his pocket and pulled out his wallet, not missing a beat with the song. He stared into his wallet, and then looked out at our congregation, who by now was watching to see how much he would pull out. I put my face in my hands.

It was a long hymn with many verses, so Mildred had time to go to each member of the work team and stand next to him during the song. Each one registered a brief shocked look, glanced out at the congregation, and fumbled with their money as they performed. Mildred, obviously pleased with the results, then went to the rest of the congregation. I felt tired.

At the end of the service, I stammered out a few strange words of thanks to the work crew and watched as they talked with their new friends during coffee hour. I noticed a rat trap underneath the table still baited with peanut butter, and I wondered if our strategy of facing the hard thing was working. But when I heard Mike and LaGuardia laughing as one of the North Carolina men asked them how they "got saved," I couldn't help but think we might be on the right track. For me, this is what the good news of Graffiti was all about—the people, through Jesus Christ, really could, like Mike said, "Be Somebody."

I'd rather be with people I know and don't like
than with people I don't know and don't like.
—MEMBER OF OUR BIBLE STUDY GROUP

c h a p t e r seven

The Most Respected Man in the Neighborhood

No matter how many blessings God gave us—alcoholics who stopped drinking because they accepted Christ or abandoned buildings that got repaired because of generous work teams—I quickly realized that some things on the Lower East Side never seemed to change. Rents continued to be unaffordable, forcing more and more people to live on the streets or in Tompkins Square Park. Jobs continued to be hard to find, forcing many into increasingly desperate situations. And drugs continued to be readily available, forcing hundreds of individuals into lifestyles that affected both their housing and their jobs.

On the block where Graffiti sat, Luis was the sole supplier of both crack and "employment" for most of our neighbors. If people needed a quick fix or a couple of bucks, a bag of "good stuff" or a chance to earn a "good income," they knew they could count on Luis, the short, muscle-toned man who lived with his wife and three children in an apartment in the middle of the block. If anyone dared to disrupt the steady flow of traffic and business that hurried down our street, well, they would deal with Luis or one of his men. He was a normal fixture in the neighborhood.

The very first week after my arrival in the neighborhood, someone told me about Luis. In fact, during the next several years, I never stopped hearing about him. As if he were their small-town hero, people loved talking about the Puerto Rican guy who has a black belt in Karate. Others would joke and tell me, "Luis is the one who keeps crime off our streets." I heard over and over again how "if it weren't for Luis, I'd be in trouble." Whether it was paying their light bill or protecting their block, most people who knew him said he ran the neighborhood. It seemed as if Luis was the most respected man in the community.

That's what Bill told me the day we stood outside the church and I asked him what he thought of this character. The tall African American music director, who'd been a part of Graffiti since I first came, glanced up and down Seventh as I asked his opinion. Since Bill lived in an abandoned building across the street, he had always felt responsible for teaching me what he knew. When he heard my question, though, he looked at me as if he needed to prepare me: "I guess you could say he looks out for the families on this street. He keeps his word. He keeps our street safe."

There was no doubt Luis was a natural leader whom everyone looked up to, a sincere yet firm man who looked you in the eye when he talked with you. He often taught karate lessons to the children in the neighborhood, took them to tournaments, and made sure they were taken care of. If he wanted a bottle of water, he'd pick one of the kids to run to the store for him and then pay him thirty dollars for "doing Luis a favor." He was always respectful of everyone when he spoke, wore creased khaki pants and tight T-shirts that showed every well-defined muscle, and walked with an authority and pride I had rarely seen before. Where I came from in Oklahoma, only coaches, teachers, or preachers exhibited that kind of authority.

"If every six-year-old knows what he does, why isn't he arrested?" I asked Bill as we stood in front of our storefront.

Bill shifted uneasily and sipped his coffee. He was a gracious man with a soft heart. He did not like talking unkindly about others if he didn't have to. "Well, the cops do come from time to time, but they never arrest *him*. See, he looks out for the churches, too, you know. He always makes sure that *your* place is safe. No one breaks into a car or a storefront on *this* block." Bill gestured up and down the pavement, pointing to parked cars, chained bicycles, and barred windows.

"But, Bill, what do *you* think of him?"

He held his gaze, then sighed. "One time some guys living in an abandoned building came into a Bible study we had. Their faces were bloody, and they said Luis's men had gone over there to drive them out. One guy got hit with a tire iron. The whole thing made me pretty uncomfortable."

I could understand why, I told him, remembering another situation that one of our homeless friends told me about a few days before. Sam had been having a particularly rough week on the streets, and his hair, face, and clothes showed it. As he turned the corner to come to Graffiti's storefront, he was approached by some of Luis's men, telling him to keep moving, that someone who "looked so shaggy and pathetic" was not welcome here. Sam tried to explain that he was coming to the church for a meal and some new clothes, but they wouldn't listen to him. Finally, they threatened Sam to "get going or else." So he did.

Bill continued his lesson for me: "Some years he has a party for everyone here on this block. He has hamburgers, steaks, hot dogs . . . everything free. He even has a live band. You name it. It's like a public relations thing. I stay away from it. I don't mess with that stuff." Bill finished with a final glare at me that I interpreted as a warning. I nodded to my friend and watched him walk toward the park.

The funny thing about Luis, though, was that by all external appearances, he lived what seemed to be a normal life. He had a nice apartment on the block, wouldn't allow drugs in his home, and was extremely protective of his son and daughters, not allowing them even to attend programs at Graffiti because he thought the other children there would have a bad influence on them. He kept his promises to people, and though he was arguably the "King of Seventh Street," he did not seem to notice how deadly his work was. People were becoming desperate for heroine or crack, getting their supply from Luis and then coming to us for food at the church or in the park because they had spent their grocery money on their habit. I thought about what, if anything, we could do.

I remembered another time when a resident who lived nearby told me of his introduction to Luis. He was walking down Seventh Street on his way to a meeting when he suddenly heard a brick crash on the sidewalk behind him. When he turned around, he realized that some of Luis's men were throwing bricks at him. He walked right up to them and asked them what they thought they were doing. Harsh words were exchanged and the resident eventually moved on. But the next day when he walked back down the street, the same men approached him with an apology and an offer of five hundred dollars to "make up for things." He was stunned, and wondered what kind of money was flowing through our street. I wondered too.

Several days later, I was on my way to the church when I happened to walk by the "most respected man" in the neighborhood. I tried not to stare, but it was hard not to notice a man at least a foot taller than Luis yelling in his face. Luis held his cool for a second, then grabbed the man's shirt collar, threw him against the wall, and—inches from his face—instructed him never to speak with him or any of his men that way again. "Understand?" Stumbling and nervous, the man whimpered away like a puppy who had just been kicked. I gulped and picked up my pace.

That night as I walked home from the church office, reflecting on the interactions I had had during the day, I was interrupted by that same short, muscle-bound Hispanic man standing alone on the sidewalk. I shuffled uneasily.

"I want to talk to you," Luis said firmly, looking me straight in the eye. I swallowed, remembering the encounter I had witnessed earlier. Obviously, I could not keep walking, so I tried to look brave.

He continued, "Listen. I'm going to be gone this summer, and I'm not going to be able to have my party for the block." I wondered what in the world that had to do with me.

He cleared his throat. "Well, I know you give a meal on Wednesday nights. So I tell you what I want to do. I want to give *you* the money I usually spend on the block party and have *you* do it up right. Buy steaks, get a band—whatever you need for your meal." He looked at me as a man accustomed to authority, expecting my easy submission.

I felt skinny and young, but managed to squeak out, "Luis, we have to talk." We agreed to meet the next evening in the empty lot beside the storefront.

The next day I gathered as much courage and prayer as I could and, at the end of the day, walked slowly to the gravel lot to wait for Luis. There were a number of junked and abandoned cars surrounding me. Long shanks of grass grew from under the flat tires of some of the older cars. The roofs of a few cars were smashed, as if some giant child had stepped on them, and the doors were rusted open. I knew my friend Larry slept in a car in the corner of the lot, his hammer safe beside him, just in case. Other men lived there, too, whom I didn't know.

It was twilight. My mouth was dry and I looked around the lot. Were some of Luis's lieutenants here? Did one of them have a tire iron or a brick ready to toss my way? I gulped, wiped my sweaty palms against my jeans, and suddenly thought about how little Luis and I had in common. I enjoyed reading poetry, going on picnics, and teaching the Bible. I imagined he was into ripping off people's noses, shooting off their kneecaps, and taking their money.

The gravel crunched as Luis came up to me. I turned and saw how serious his face was. Then he looked me in the eyes, and I went straight to the point: "Look, Luis. Would the money you give us come from dealing drugs?"

He stared at me for what seemed a long time. I tried to swallow. "You know it does," he said slowly.

I nodded and shifted my weight. For some strange reason, his honesty put me a little more at ease, and I managed to explain that we were here to share that people could leave the darkness of that life for a new life in Jesus Christ. "So, Luis, although I appreciate your offer, it just doesn't make sense for us to be funded by the biggest drug dealer in the neighborhood." Then I realized that I was saying no to the "King of Seventh Street." What would happen now?

Luis glanced at a beat-up car, then looked at me again for a long time without speaking. The silence was frightening. Finally, he leaned forward, more serious than before, and whispered, "You know, when I was in Vietnam, I told God I'd give him my life if he would just get me out of there. God did get me out of there, but when I got back to New York, well, I couldn't find a job. This is the only thing that worked out for me."

He pointed up and down the street. "But I tell you what I'm going to do. You know the boys in your boys' club? I'm going to do stuff for them, get them tickets for the World Series."

I listened to his ideas, and for some reason, I was feeling braver. "You're talking about all the things you want to do *for* God, Luis. But God doesn't need that. All he wants is your heart."

Luis gritted his jaw in determination and glanced away again. After a few more long seconds, he said, "In a year's time I'm going to give my life to Christ. Yeah, I'm going to stand before this neighborhood and tell everyone my testimony. It will change the neighborhood!"

I wasn't so sure and stepped out a little further. "You keep talking like that and it will never happen. In a year's time, something will keep you from taking the stand."

We talked for a long time in the lot until the sun was completely down and the darkness of the night surrounded us. We agreed to disagree on the money issue, though we respected each other's position and each knew the other was sincere. Still, as Luis walked into the busy night, I suddenly realized that although we were very different, we were also very much the same. How many times had I told God I was going to do something for him, somehow to earn a place at his table, and then never quite get around to it? Just like Luis, I often heard myself say, "Later," when God had come to me.

I walked home more aware than ever of my need for God's grace. But I had no idea in what direction Luis would go.

Crisis in the Park

Tensions rose in the neighborhood during the next months after my talk with Luis. He did go "out of town," and because there was no block party that summer, people on the block seemed a little resentful. By the time Luis returned, however, neighbors were back to their normal challenges and disappointments. Still, I knew we had not seen the last of Luis's influence. He and I acknowledged each other's presence as we'd pass on the street; we were both busy meeting the "needs" of our people.

For me, that meant recognizing that housing problems on the Lower East Side were not getting better; they seemed to be getting worse, and most of the conflict seemed to be coming to a head in, of all places, Tompkins Square Park. Rumors of what we had long feared were circulating up and down the surrounding shops and apartment buildings: the police were going to close the park. Real estate developers had been working hard to increase the property values of those buildings around the park, and they knew that could never happen as long as homeless people were living in the park, as long as drug addicts like Luis's clients were doing their business there. New York City's economy was getting stronger all the time, but somehow that seemed mostly to benefit those with deep pockets or big invest-ments, like real estate. Those living on the fringe were already struggling day to day, and if Tompkins Square Park were to be shut down by the city officials, we knew even more poor and homeless people would be affected or displaced. Still, other res-idents of the Lower East Side perceived it as a long overdue "cleaning up" of a public property. Any way you looked at it, it was a mess.

I decided to attend the public forum at the community board meeting to hear the various sides of the park debate. What I did not expect was to find so many emotions flying, tempers explod-ing, and agendas challenged at the meeting.

"My child picked up a hypodermic needle in the playground! We've got to do something about this," shouted a middle-aged woman with long brown hair, her hands firmly pressed on her child's shoulders.

"But what about the homeless? They have nowhere to go," responded a tall man with a long beard and round glasses. "The rent for an apartment in our neighborhood is astronomical, and the park is the only place that has any bathroom facilities. What will happen to these people if we push them out of the only place they have to stay? We are not the kind of neighborhood that pushes people out."

Another man chimed in, "Why not follow the community board's plans and renovate the park section by section? Then we can set limits for use of space in the park and not push any-one completely out. I know people are sick of the homeless. To be honest, so am I! But what we are talking about doing is totally wrong."

"But what about the children?" a neatly-trimmed man shouted out, interrupting the others.

Then I turned and noticed a group of squatters occupying the last two rows of chairs in the meeting room. They wore an assortment of leather jackets, army jackets, chains, and pins. "What about the pigs?" one of them shouted. The back two rows roared. "What about the fat pigs? They're an occupying army! The community board cowards have them posted here too. Down with racism! Down with the police army!"

"Oh, shut up!" a woman in a tan overcoat shouted from the front.

I sighed. We were going nowhere fast. At that point, the chairperson began to hammer the table with his gavel as the room exploded into shouting matches. He was calling on the group to discuss this reasonably, trying to yell over the crowd for order. I noticed a policeman at the door put his walkie-talkie to his mouth and whisper something. Everyone was shouting around me. I sank down in my chair and watched, wanting to put my hands over my ears. No one was listening; no agenda was even introduced, let alone discussed; and certainly no consensus was going to be reached. After about thirty minutes more of continuing chaos, I had had enough and got up to leave. I walked out the back door still hearing shouts and accusations and questions flying around the room. This was not an easy situation.

I walked back to the park, which was about ten blocks from the meeting, but I didn't really want to talk to anybody. Instead, I stood and stared at the park from across the street, trying to see it as if for the first time. There were sidewalks and iron fences and trees with birds sitting on the branches. But that was about the only thing that resembled a park. Packed across the rest of the space were strange little structures, some made out of cardboard and blankets, some with wooden poles and plastic cloths draped as protection from the rain. Some had mattresses made into walls. Music was blaring everywhere. A few people had fires going in front of their shacks. Newspapers, beer cans, and empty pizza cartons littered the benches. A rat hurried across the street in front of me. Though it was once a spacious park that spanned about five blocks, it suddenly seemed small, crowded, and very sad. I was staring at a shantytown in the middle of New York City in the spring of 1991.

"Hey, Pastor!" Tommy had seen me staring and came up to me in his wheelchair, his faithful dog, Sirius, by his side. Tommy had been stabbed in a gang fight many years ago and couldn't use his legs, but somehow he never seemed to lose his goodwill.

"We've been enjoying the evening. Isn't it nice weather?" He patted Sirius and grinned at me, his middle-aged face looking young again. "See, if you look up through the trees in the park, you can see the stars." He pointed up. I followed Tommy's finger, and sure enough, there were three or four stars visible beyond the trees.

Tommy didn't know what else to say to me; he had always been more of a listener than a talker. I sat down on a park bench, and we looked out together at the separate groups of activity. Sirius sat beside her master. To my right, I saw Junior and Martha fighting out in front of their tent. Though they didn't use drugs anymore, they did want to get married and find a decent place to stay. They were frequently a part of our Bible study and were asking a lot of questions about God. A few feet from them stood a group of rowdy men around a fire in a trash can; they were drinking and talking and feeding the flames with boards. Closer to us, a man I had met years ago was playing the bongos. A crowd of people circled Luigi, swaying to his beat, and watching his hands pound out a rhythm that was both loud and constant. Others joined him beating plastic buckets or big tin cans. Some people were walking from hut to hut, like neighbors in a village in some far-off developing country. But I was not overseas; I was in the middle of the biggest city in the wealthiest nation in the world. And though I certainly didn't want anyone to have to live like this, I knew that this *was* home to many of these people. The thought of seeing them forced out was both troubling and painful.

I stood up. I thanked Tommy for pointing out the stars to me that night and mumbled something about people deserving better. As Tommy started rolling his wheelchair down the sidewalk, his kind, dark face looked up into mine. "Don't worry. This won't last long, Pastor," he said as he joined his friends in the park.

I hoped he was right.

Preparing for the Worst

The next day I received a phone call from a priest who cared for a parish across the street. New York's newspapers and television news programs were reporting on the "growing tensions in Tompkins Square Park," suggesting that residents and city officials were preparing for the worst. I had been wrestling with how those of us in the religious community would—or should—respond. So I listened carefully on the telephone to the priest's words.

"We're faxing our request a second time to the mayor. All the pastors and priests in the neighborhood have signed it, and we are requesting an emergency meeting with him," he spoke with an urgency I hadn't heard in his voice before. He was worried that the real estate people had convinced the new mayor that he needed to close the park so they could proceed with their development plans. The priest believed that would be a tragedy for the community.

"Our community board has worked four years to put together a plan that would renovate the park section by section so that we won't drive out people who have no place to go. Our council member is adamantly opposed to closing the park," the priest told me. I didn't have to remind him that every elected representative from our community had publicly protested the park's closing. I asked him how the mayor could even consider closing it.

"Because he's the mayor, Taylor. They're playing politics with people's lives." I agreed to sign the request and thanked the priest for his call. This park incident was getting more and more serious. I prayed God would somehow intervene before a disaster occurred. And I waited.

That night Junior and Martha, our Bible study regulars who lived in the park, came and rang the buzzer of our apartment. They seemed panicked. I wondered what had happened.

"The mayor's deputy is in the park right now talking to the homeless," they said at the same time. Their eyes grew wide with fear. "Something's going on. The rumor is they're going to close the park tomorrow."

I hurried with Junior and Martha back to the park, passing a few of Luis's men doing business with some men who looked familiar, and I wondered how they could be so callused about what was happening in their own backyard. I followed Junior toward the crowd, which by now had gathered into an uneasy circle. I stood in the background. Sure enough, a police deputy was trying to negotiate with the nervous group of homeless folks as well as the anarchists who had begun rallying around the park's homeless population since they first heard of the con-flict. I looked across the group and tried to listen.

"We just want to find a peaceful solution. We just want to give you other options." The deputy spoke calmly and confidently; as the mayor's top level executive, he was used to this sort of situation.

"We don't want any trouble," Junior shouted out from the back of the crowd. "We just want a place to stay. I'm not going to a shelter. The last time I went to the shelter, they jumped me before I was even admitted. Four guys. They not only took my wallet. They took my *shoes!* I'm not putting Martha through any of that!"

"I understand your problems," the deputy continued. A few other police officers stepped closer to him as if to guard him. "But there are larger issues too. We really don't want anyone to get hurt here."

Luigi, the bongo player, responded, "We don't want any prob-lems either, man. We just want a place to stay. And we're *not* going to any damn shelter with its drugs and TB."

As the deputy talked, I looked into the faces of Junior and Martha, Tommy, and Luigi. Suddenly, I thought about every other face I had encountered since I had come here: Paul, Bill, LaGuardia and Mike, George, Peggy, and the others; how God had used them in my life to teach me of his mercy and grace. We had grown together, and now it felt like our very community was being threatened. These were my friends, and when I saw how scared they really were, scared for their lives, I knew I had to do something. I remembered the priest's words earlier on the phone: "You can't fight for every issue. You've got to choose your battle."

When I looked at the scared faces of my friends, something became crystal clear to me. I thought about the abandoned buildings and the people living in them. I thought about the little tents made out of plastic. I realized: *This is my issue. These are my people, and they are about to lose their homes.*

The deputy dismissed the crowd, mumbling something about doing whatever the mayor and his officers said. I walked slowly back to my apartment, passing a woman who had just shot up with heroine she had probably bought from Luis. Where was he now? Who really were the most respected men in this neighborhood? Who had the power and the authority to change people's lives, to order where they lived and worked? I had often said in Bible study that Jesus was above every principality and power. He didn't seem to be visibly evident in these hardball politics. What was this about?

Back in our living room, Susan and I talked about what was about to happen. We prayed together and asked God to help us and our friends through this crisis. Then I picked up the phone and called my supervisor within our denominational structure. When she asked me what was the matter, I sighed a deep breath and told her, "I think I may get arrested tomorrow. I wanted to call and let you know tonight."

"It's gotten that bad there? Well, thanks for letting me know," she said in a matter-of-fact manner. "Be sure to read your missionary personnel manual and see what the consequences may be." She knew the decision was up to me.

"Thanks," I answered as I set down the receiver. I set my alarm for five o'clock in the morning and went to bed. But the next morning, I realized I must have done something wrong— the alarm went off at four o'clock instead! I was wide awake now, lying on my back, and staring into the darkness—still wondering about power and respect and authority.

chapter eight
Busted

By 4:30 A.M., I pulled myself out of bed, poured a bowl of cereal, and listened to the quiet of the building. My mind picked through a variety of emotions and thoughts. At first I felt like a person who was about to step off the end of a high diving board for the first time. Then I questioned again whether this was completely ridiculous and foolish; after all, I said to myself, I'm not the kind of person who goes to jail, or even thinks about doing the things that get you there. Was this stupid? Was I putting myself or my family at risk by standing with our homeless friends in the park? But I kept coming back to the image of the night before, the stunned, scared looks on the faces of the people as they listened to the deputy. These *are* my people, human beings who are my friends. This was their home, and this was their issue. They were vulnerable and did not have many choices. No, I knew I had to join them today.

125

I walked over to the park in the darkness just before dawn, still nervous, yet still firm in what I was about to do. The streets were quiet, and I could hear the birds singing. A rat scurried behind a trash can on the sidewalk as the squirrels in the park were just about to send the rats into hiding during the daylight. I was expectant, but I wasn't exactly sure of what. Then I saw Tommy, Martha, Junior, Luigi, and the others, all wide awake and all waiting. Young nose-pierced anarchists and other political activists had joined them this early morning, many of whom didn't normally stay in the park. Those who had come for the confrontation talked excitedly in small groups, trying to second-guess what might happen. Those who actually lived in the park also wanted the latest news, but their eyes were wider and there was more fear in their chatter. I joined my friends and stood beside Tommy, talking, praying. Waiting.

Handcuffed

Within minutes of being there, I saw one of the young anarchists ride up on his bicycle, shouting, "They're coming from Twenty-third Street! About five hundred cops, and they've got hundreds of vehicles!"

"Tell the church to start ringing the church bells!" yelled one of the priests who had gathered with the people.

Junior and Martha started throwing their possessions in a cart. "We've got to get out of here," he exclaimed, tossing blankets and bags into an old grocery cart. "We can't have any trouble."

A small man with long, stringy hair took a metal bar and began to bang the iron fence to alert everyone. Luigi sat on a bench next to his bongos, then jumped up, then sat back down again and screamed, "This makes me so mad!" Tommy just sat in his wheelchair patting his dog, staring at the nervous activity and saying nothing.

All across the park, people started pulling their most important possessions together. The church bells began to ring. Some spiked-haired anarchist with a bullhorn instructed us: "All right! Make your choices on how you wish to resist! Choose your places! Remember, the power belongs to the people! This is nothing but an occupying force, and we don't have to accept this!" Everyone's adrenaline was flowing, and for the first time in my life, I felt just a tiny portion of what it might feel like having an army march toward you to take over your home, your town, your life. You dread the noise of the invasion as the troops get closer, fearing that life will never again be the same. This felt like war. My friends were about to have their homes taken away, and I was scared.

A few minutes later, busloads of police rolled up on all sides of the park. They were very organized, surrounding the park with trucks, cars, and all types of vehicles, systematically closing the park. A police officer announced over another bullhorn (that was louder than the anarchist's) how the park was now officially closed, and everyone in it should please leave immediately. Police officers on motorcycles or on foot went section by section throughout the park, closing each with barricades as they went along.

Their strategy was quick, careful, and precise; apparently, they did not want a repeat of the riot of 1988 that occurred in the park for many of the same reasons. On that dark night, young anarchists dressed in grunge attire had rebelled against curfews the police had imposed on the homeless people squatting in and around the park. Their agenda had been to resist the authority and support the use of the park for the homeless, not the real estate developers. Instead, pandemonium broke out, and later, more than one hundred charges of abuse by the police drew enormous—and unwelcome—publicity. I learned about the whole thing the day after it had occurred; for some reason, I slept right through the riot the night before!

This time the police responded differently. Within ten minutes, emergency trucks, motorcycles, official cars, and park and sanitation trucks rolled up, surrounded the entire park, and sealed any entrance or exit. When I saw how quickly they took over, I realized that if my alarm clock hadn't gone off when it did, I would have been forced to stay outside of the park.

The police then sealed off the section where we were and calmly moved blue wooden barricades around us. Squatters and anarchists shouted obscenities at them. Within minutes, the media arrived in full force, little vans with massive antennae on them. The priest held an impromptu press conference a few feet from us, and I sat with Tommy, who was holding his dog's collar so as not to lose him in the chaos. Tommy had sometimes come to our Bible study, so I knew how sensitive he was and how difficult this would be for him. As the camera and lights shone on the priest, I watched tears run down Tommy's cheeks.

"This is worse than taking away someone's apartment," he whispered to me, "because this is our whole life. This is the whole neighborhood's life, where so many people spend their day. Now it's closed."

A familiar-looking newsman must have noticed Tommy's tears. He walked right up to him, thrusting a microphone in his face. I stared incredulously as he asked my friend, "Why are you crying?"

Tommy paused. Then he looked into the eyes of this polished reporter and said, "Why are you *not* crying?"

Before the reporter had a chance to answer, the police again announced over the loudspeaker that anyone who did not leave the park would immediately be placed under arrest. A few people carried their belongings past us and out onto the street. Tommy and I did not move. The camera crew stepped back.

A tall white policeman with broad shoulders approached me and asked me if I was going to leave the park. I said no. Then he asked me if I was going to resist arrest, and again I said no. So he took my arms, pulled them gently behind my back, and slid hard plastic handcuffs around my wrists. He led me inside a small paddy wagon that had just pulled up. When they shut the door, the paddy wagon was completely dark. I wondered about Susan who was at home, probably watching this on television.

Though I couldn't see him, I recognized the voice of Luigi inside the wagon. He was talking nonstop about what it was like getting booked at the different police stations, talking as if he was going to a picnic. "This will be easy," he spoke into the darkness. "What is hard is when they take you to Central Booking. That's the closest thing to hell I've ever seen. There you sit in a huge room with all these other guys on the concrete floor for fourteen hours with your hands cuffed like this. Guys are throwing up and going through withdrawal. Hey! Where are we going, anyway?" He shouted to the police.

The door opened up again. The little paddy wagon was flooded with light and the chaotic noise of the police, protesters, and reporters all yelling. Two police officers loaded Tommy into the paddy wagon, wheelchair and all. A friend had taken Sirius, his dog. I could see smoke where homeless folks had set fire to their own possessions so the police wouldn't take them. The door slammed again, leaving us in the dark. At first, neither of us felt like talking, though Luigi kept at it. There was a heavy sense of defeat that the police really were doing what they had said they would, in spite of protests by elected officials and local residents. That's when Tommy and I began to talk. Quietly, we talked about issues we felt were important: taking a stand, appreciating the things you have. I didn't know if that short conversation would be the seed he needed to rededicate his life to Christ; I only hoped it would.

My feelings had moved suddenly from defeat to relief because at least now I knew that something was happening. The uncertainty of the day before as well as this morning standing in the park was more frightening than knowing I'd be arrested. Still, I knew I was one of the lucky ones; I, at least, was a white male minister. People assumed that the police sometimes went easier on guys like me. This would merely be uncomfortable for me, unlike some of the others. Because Tommy was African American with a history of arrests—he had other confrontations with the police for the closing of squats or gang-related incidents—we both knew he might face a tougher time. In our neighborhood, the perception was that the police were more likely to harass minorities and keep them locked up longer. I tried to scan the five or so other dark faces in the wagon and realized it might not be easy for them either.

We rode around in the dark for an hour. At the precinct headquarters, my picture was taken, my fingerprints were recorded, and I was charged with "refusing to leave public property." They took my shoelaces and my belt, and shuffled me into a cell with a guy who was already fast asleep. I didn't know where Tommy or the others were taken. By this time my survival instinct kicked in, and I felt my palms sweat as I realized I was in a tiny cell with someone I didn't know. I could only imagine why he was locked up. I didn't know how long I was going to be there, and I had no idea what was happening to anyone else at the park. Still, I knew I had been fortunate, that the police were not threatening. As I sat on the bunk and waited, I was hoping Susan wasn't worrying.

My cellmate woke up to ask me what was happening, and then went back to sleep. Soon after, I was released. When I called Susan to let her know I was fine and on my way home, I noticed the red lines on my wrists from the handcuffs. I hopped on the subway, walked into our tiny apartment (which was looking better than usual) and took Susan back over to the park. It was officially closed, all our friends had dispersed, and the police had invaded the area. They were building ten-foot-high fences around the park so no one could enter, and there were clusters of blue uniforms on each corner. As we walked into a pizza shop, we even noticed dozens of police officers still on the roofs of nearby apartment buildings.

I still didn't know where Tommy was. I looked for him all around the park, but it was totally sealed off. Demonstrators were still shouting, and TV cameras still rolling. That would be a common sight for the next few months as the park remained officially closed. But Tommy was nowhere to be seen.

Several weeks later, my friend Tommy finally found me as I happened to be walking past the demonstrators and police at the park. He chose his words carefully. "I've been thinking about a lot of things," he said slowly. "I've already stopped using. I want to . . . start again. I want to, how do you say it? I want to rededicate my life. I'll be there at your place on Sunday. Do you have a couple of guys who can lift my chair down into the basement where you said you meet?" Behind him, an anarchist waved a homemade flag and shouted obscenities at the police.

"This is getting weird," Tommy said.

"Attack" Sheep

For months, the park's closing was a sensitive subject in our neighborhood. Most believed—like I did—that there were a lot of other ways the police could have responded to the growing crisis rather than act like a military force and invade it. News reports sold it as a positive way to "clean up" the neighborhood, but many of us knew it came at the expense of homeless and poor people. Many believed it communicated to these same people that their government was not for them, but rather against them. While I had always grown up thinking police officers were there to serve and protect, many neighbors of mine felt otherwise. Whether due to a language barrier, one bad cop, or a hundred other negative encounters, they perceived police not as friends but as invaders to avoid. For me and the people I worked with, the park's closing and the ensuing discussions were a lesson in hardball politics, where the carefully tuned machine of real estate brokers, politicians, and economic movers and shakers began to roll over anyone who got in its way.

The park wouldn't reopen for almost two years. Rather than addressing the issues of the homeless, the city spent millions of dollars on major renovations and security. But to our amazement, they also did not shut the entire park: they did manage to leave open a long narrow stretch known as "the dog run" so those who lived in the wealthier apartment building across the street could walk their dogs.

When the "new" Tompkins Square Park finally did reopen, we noticed shorter benches that people could not lie on and wider sidewalks so police cars could drive on them. It was a clear message about who this park was for.

Still, as a result of my getting "busted," something else happened. I began to notice a peculiar bond surface with folks as we continued our meal outreach. (Our FLIP program—Free Lunch In the Park—had to be changed to FLOP—Free Lunch Outside the Park.) At the Bible study, people began to perceive me as "one of them." As a result, I was finding myself with more opportunities to get involved in the daily lives of the neighborhood people. What I did not yet realize, though, was that more time with people meant more demands on me. I was getting tired.

During the year following the park's closing, I found myself running out of steam. One day a friend loaned me a car so my family and I could get out of the city. We had made our way to a nature center and were soaking in the sunshine. Susan noticed some sheep grazing alongside a chain-link fence, but when she reached through to touch the wool of a sheep's head, the sheep butted its head against the fence where Susan was standing and bleated out a loud *Baaaa*.

"Whoa!" Susan said and jumped back. The sheep slammed against the fence again. "That must be an *attack* sheep!" We laughed and went to the next exhibit.

I was glad we were having a break. I told my wife that I was beginning to think life in the city was getting to me. "I feel like something that's spread too thin, or like a cake that has gone flat," I said, rubbing the back of my neck and staring at the deer. I took a full deep breath. Susan made sure we stayed at the nature center for a long, relaxed day.

But by the next Saturday I was back at the edge of the park giving out sandwiches. The sight of the ten-foot fence that now surrounded Tompkins Square Park, the policemen guarding it, and the protesters picketing discouraged me. It didn't help that summer temperatures were nearing the nineties. As I looked down the street, I could see a smoggy haze and more than two hundred people lined up to get a sandwich.

Doug, a man who had started fights around our mission before, somehow got behind the table with the people handing out sandwiches. He started throwing sandwiches to his friends in the line. When the others standing in line saw the inequity of the flying sandwiches, two hundred bodies twisted and began to rumble, like some huge animal. These hungry people looked ready to attack the tables and capture their own food at any price. Everyone was hot. Some had been drinking. Everyone was angry, and I knew we were in trouble.

"Doug, come over here and let me talk to you," I said firmly. Doug sneered at me with fury, his forehead glossy in the summer heat. I explained to him that we couldn't start the meal until he and I had a chance to talk.

"I'm staying here," Doug blurted out, and with the same animosity, he grabbed a gray metal box cutter from his pocket. He pushed the blade forward and held it out in front of him, ready to slash anyone who came near him. I'd seen other people pull out knives, but they had only used them to intimidate. Doug's temper seemed hot enough that I felt he might use it.

I tried to speak calmly, encouraging our volunteers to move slowly away from the table so Doug and I could talk. As they did, Doug stood still, holding the blade, eyes raging.

"Now you have some room, Doug. Let's get away from here and talk," I said, trying to reassure him—and myself.

The lady serving next to Doug, eyes as big as frying pans by now, stepped quietly away from the table. Doug still wouldn't budge. The line of people writhed and coiled with tension. Everyone was sweating. Time seemed to have stopped in the summer heat. When Doug finally did approach me, his eyes darted around from the ground to the fence to the line of people waiting for a sandwich. His blade flashed in the July sun.

"You embarrassed me," Doug hissed at me like an angry cat.

"Well, I'm sorry I embarrassed you, but we need your help in other ways today. Now put the knife up, first of all, and let's go over here and talk." I was desperate.

"I'll cut you up," Doug spat out the words, and then he began to dance and jump about as if he were a boxer in the ring, still thrusting the blade toward me. I kept trying to talk him away from the crowd, but he kept up his dance. Soon, my friend Bill came and stood beside me like a bodyguard. When he saw Bill, Doug began to run around in the street, swinging his blade, and screaming at the people. A few backed away, others ignored him, and some even yelled obscenities back at him. I sighed.

"Stay here, Bill," I said. I walked to a phone booth twenty feet away and dialed 911. I'd never had to call the police before in my life. My heart felt like a chunk of lead. By the time I came back to the sandwich line, Doug had run down the street, still swinging his arms and shouting at me. At least he was away from the crowd, I thought. At least we could begin our meal. (A block away, the police finally caught him.)

After swallowing a few bites of bologna and bread, I sat down on the stoop for a moment and tried to process what I was feeling. Fatigue most of all. Anger at Doug's obnoxious behavior. Failure because I had to call the police. Dullness. The more I thought about it, the more I realized I did not have enough energy to feel much of anything. Whenever someone had come to me recently asking for help or food or for money, I found myself reacting suspiciously, thinking, *Yeah, yeah, I've heard that before.* In other areas of my life, there also seemed to be conflict. A litany of examples flooded my mind. Earlier that week, I helped at a funeral for a young man who lived on our street. One of the people at the graveside took a swing at the funeral director.

Before the coffin was lowered, the director said, "I don't have to put up with this." He got in his hearse and drove off, leaving some of the family and me stranded in the cemetery.

The Sunday before that a woman in church had confronted me publicly about a church policy she disagreed with, and almost everyone who heard her immediately took sides. A tense murmuring rose throughout the room, and I couldn't help but wonder, *Am I doing the right thing?* Some other pastor or leader, I was sure, would have been much wiser.

A month or so earlier, I had stood on the stairway in a tenement building between an angry, drug-addicted man and his terrified girlfriend. She had finally kicked him out of her apartment, called me to come help her, and now he was trying to get back upstairs to brutalize her, to show her who was "in charge." For some reason, I was literally in between them, trying to mediate between two troubled lovers. When the boyfriend had had enough of my talking, he suddenly pushed me and began swinging wildly, punching me over and over in the chest, the head, and the shoulders, to get me out of the way. His girlfriend screamed for him to stop.

Finally he did, and he stormed out of the building. I stood on the stairs, rasping with each breath. My heart pounded against the walls of my chest. *I'm too old for this,* I kept thinking.

While I sat on the stoop that hot summer day after the Doug incident, scanning the events of the past couple of months, every part of my body felt as heavy as lead. I glanced at the sky, hoping for some reprieve. Instead, out of nowhere, Andy sat down beside me. Andy was a man who was angry at specific Christians, angry at the church in general, angry at his family, angry at the world. He didn't even say hello when he sat on the stoop; he just started right in.

"I'm so mad. I can't get a job. I'm fed up! God has done *noth-ing* for me. *Nothing!* Do you hear me?" He was working himself into a frenzy. All I could do was stare at him. As he continued rambling, he reached into his backpack and pulled out a huge annotated Scofield Bible. He held it in his hand like a missile, and in one sudden movement, he flung it over his shoulder with all his might. The Bible flew into the air about twenty or thirty feet. As it descended, it seemed to gain speed. I noticed it was heading straight toward poor Mr. Ferguson, our thin, gentle neighbor, who was simply trying to dump his trash.

"Look out!" I shouted. Mr. Ferguson looked up in time to see a deadly black object speeding toward him. He kicked over a trash can and made a dive for the side. The Scofield Bible hit the wall beside him like a cannonball. *Boom!*—it sounded lethal, and dropped to the ground with a thud.

"I'm sorry!" I exclaimed from the stoop and glared at Andy who by this time was walking down the street, oblivious to what he had just done. Is this the kind of evangelism I dreamed of? Threatening gentle neighbors with projectiles of the Word? Breaking up fights on the street and in stairwells? Was this why I was called here?

I sat back down on the stoop, feeling completely incompe-tent and exhausted. Again I looked down the street. It was bleached of any joy or even interest for me. I had a cough that wouldn't go away, it was hotter than I could ever remember, and I was aching all over. I felt empty, abandoned, and worst of all, hated. I don't think I had ever realized how hard it was to be hated, how much it affected your whole being. I knew that most of the time I was merely the lightning rod for the much deeper anger of those around me. But even if the animosity was aimed at me unfairly, the anger of others had pierced my heart deeply, like multiple knife wounds. I stared at the ground and remembered a line I had read recently in a book by Eberhard Arnold, "Pain is a plow that tears up the heart and makes it open to the truth." I did not feel open; I felt torn.

Rock Bottom

By the time the summer was almost over, I was too tired to move. One Thursday afternoon, I was working from home and had almost finished for the day. I just needed to make one more phone call, so I dialed the telephone number of Annabel to see how she was doing.

"Listen!" Annabel shouted at me with a thick accent over the phone. I wasn't exactly ready for more yelling. She continued, "I have had a *terrible* time. You don't know! I was in the hospital, and they didn't treat me right." Annabel had been coming regularly to our church for some time and was faithful to the ministry. I asked her to explain what happened at the hospital.

"They put a needle in my knee, a *big* needle. Oh, it hurt so bad. They tried to put it in deeper but I was so mad, I kicked the doctor. I didn't mean to, but I kicked him right in the private parts." Because I was exhausted, I couldn't help but laugh. She didn't seem to notice and went on. "Everybody crowded around him. But I said, 'Hey! Don't worry about *his* pain. What about *my* pain?' I told the doctor, 'Sir, I didn't *mean* to kick you in the private parts, but if you come close to me, so help me God, I will kick you in the *same place* again!'"

My wife noticed me shaking in my chair as I listened. I was laughing and crying at the same time, I was so tired. The image of a hospital staff in an operating room, crowding around the poor doctor doubled over with pain, with a woman shouting at them to forget about his pain, was too much for me. I felt a wave of admiration for her because she would not succumb to whatever had been done to her; she would fight if it hurt, and she would stand up for her rights. I was also glad I was her pastor and not her doctor.

Annabel finished her story. "They wouldn't come near me. They kept that needle in me for *three* hours. They finally roped my arms and my legs down and took it out. It was *terrible.* They have *no* respect."

I hung up the phone and explained to Susan what had happened. My two boys began to wrestle in the other room, and I could hear furniture hitting the floor. Susan asked me to go into the other room to mediate. I looked her in the eye and, half seriously, half facetiously, said, "What about *my* pain?" We both laughed as I walked into the room, but I knew that the eagerness to go on had drained from me, day by day. I was a vessel with a leak.

I went on vacation, hoping the rest might do me good and give me some time to regain perspective. Instead, the night I returned from my vacation, I found myself deathly ill, lying in our loft bed, praying for the night to be over. Everything ached, and there was no break from the agony. Susan called the doctor.

"The doctor thinks you have pneumonia," she said, wiping my brow. "We might have to take you to the hospital tomorrow if you're not better." I heard her words, but could barely respond before I closed my eyes, trying to fall back asleep. I'd never had a fever this high before.

"Oh, God, help me get through the night," I whispered and waited for what felt like an hour. I glanced at the clock again. Two minutes had passed. The aching and sweating continued.

I shut my eyes again, and in my mind's eye I saw a man standing before me. It wasn't a dream because I was still awake. Yet everything seemed intense and real, like a dream. I suppose the high fever made everything I thought take on a heightened clarity and significance. I was conscious, but what I seemed to see felt far more real than a daydream. I felt as though I was seeing it with the eyes of my heart.

The man was standing beside a stream. I could hear the stream gurgling and bubbling. The water was clearer than any water I had ever seen, and the sky above was bluer than any blue I had ever seen. All around the man there was rich deep grass as green as if it had just rained, and everywhere I looked the colors were delicious. I could hear birds singing, clearly and true, as if it were early morning. Everything was soaked in golden sunlight.

The man stood there on the path, laughing. But it was a laughter that included me. He beckoned me to go with him. He had a beard and long hair and eyes that twinkled.

"Just walk with me," he said. Somehow, I saw myself walking with him and listening to the bubbling brooks. With every step I took, I seemed to grow stronger.

Jesus (I realized who he was) looked at the birds and the stream and he laughed again.

"There's so much you don't know," he said softly to me.

For some reason, my mind moved into another realm, and I instantly grabbed hold of a thought: human beings are creatures with incredibly limited knowledge. We sin, we hurt people, and we don't usually intend to. Every movement we make brings damage and misunderstanding as we bump against each other. That's why forgiveness is not optional. God gave us forgiveness as a gift so that we could survive each other. Forgiving suddenly seemed a precious commodity.

At one point along our path, we came across a cluster of twelve-foot poles. Somehow in this fevered reality, I knew what they were. They were all my grievances and grudges. Each pole was labeled with one of the harmful things someone had done to me in the past several months. There were a lot of them, and they were clearly marked.

Jesus didn't seem to mind. He grinned at me. "OK," he said. "I'll help you carry these if you really want to. But you don't have to carry them."

As soon as I put three or four on my shoulders, they began to feel cumbersome. I could hardly turn up on the path. It suddenly seemed silly and stupid even to try to continue carrying them. When I tossed them by the side of the stream, we both laughed.

Later in the night, with my vivid feverish imagination still active, I saw myself hang gliding with Jesus and visiting a castle. Then we were hiking with a friend in the Grand Canyon and resting with our feet in a waterfall. A moment later, we were walking in the Swiss Alps with my brother. We went together back into my childhood, and I remembered names I thought I had long forgotten. When I became pompous or acted grown-up, Jesus laughed at me.

I once again saw and felt the streams, the sky, the mountains, and the sunlight as if I were a teenager. I looked toward Jesus and he shrugged. "I'll go with you as long as you want," he said. "It's that kind of walk."

Dawn finally crept into my room. My fever had broken, and I found myself feeling a little stronger. Something strange had happened in the night, something that still felt a little fuzzy to me, but I somehow felt encouraged in a way I had not felt for a long, long time. I knew I would not have to go to the hospital that morning.

The sacrifice acceptable to God
is a broken spirit.
—PSALM 51:17 NRSV

chapter
nine
Losing Ground

Although I didn't have to go to the hospital that next morning, I learned that soon I would have to go for someone else. Bill—the man who had led music for our services, who had taught me about Luis, the park, and the neighborhood—was dying. He had been in and out of the hospital with recurring health problems since I first met him, and he had always been thin and delicate. But now Bill was gaunt, his lips dry and cracked; his usually kind eyes were now wide with fear, like a horse caught in a fire. From his nose and his arm ran several plastic tubes attached to IVs. Even breathing had become difficult for him. Machines— not people—formed a circle around him. The nurses and doctors were busy with other people who were just as sick. So Bill lay in a corner room of a New York City hospital comforted only by machines. His eyes searched the ceiling in pain and fear.

"It was before God really started changing my life," Bill had told me intently one afternoon while we walked through the neighborhood. "It must have happened when I was together with Jack and living in that abandoned building on Eighth Street. I never used needles, and Jack was the only man I have ever been with. He must have given me AIDS." Bill's voice had been matter-of-fact that day, as if he were talking about music or the weather.

But tonight, as I poked my head into his hospital room and sat beside him, he could not speak matter-of-factly. He could barely speak at all. The vibrant compassionate man who had befriended me since I first came to the Lower East Side had been reduced to a frail, lifeless body. I tried to smile as I sat down, though I wasn't sure he even recognized me. Then he mumbled something barely audible. I leaned closer. "Water," he rasped, looking both at me and through me at the same time. I squeezed his hand.

I walked down the hospital corridor, past rooms of other lonely people hooked up to other machines, trying to find some container for water. I wiped my forehead, still feeling weak myself from my own illness, but somehow I also felt God was with me—and with my friend Bill. Finally, I found a nurse at the nurse's station and asked if I could bring some water to room 404.

The nurse looked at her chart and kept working. "He's not allowed to have any water," she said sternly. "Doctor's orders." I stared at her, not certain if I had really heard her correctly but feeling ignorant of any proper medical procedures. What patient would be denied water in a hospital? I was confused. I wanted her to come with me to see Bill, to see the thoughtful but delicate man I had known for the past six years, to look at his hollow eyes, to see his cracked lips. She did not respond.

"Could I bring him a little ice then?" I pressed her. "He's really in a bad way."

She pointed to a place where I could get ice and kept working. "Just a little," she said.

I carried the ice back to Bill's room, passing the other rooms of patients with AIDS. Few people in our ministry had support groups, families to see them, wives or husbands, children or parents who would take them back after encountering the debilitating effects of this horrible disease. Friends like Bill simply went into the hospital for temporary treatment and then were sent back out onto the street where they would usually disappear. Too many times, I had heard that someone had died on the street. Sometimes the hospital could find a member of the family to bury him or her. Most times they couldn't. As a result, we often held memorial services in the storefront for these friends from the street, sometimes not even knowing the full name of the person who had died. As I led the services, I could only refer to them as they were known on the street: "Smitty" or "Indio" or "Alaska."

I suppose Bill was fortunate. We knew his full name; we also knew the songs he loved, the help he offered, the heart he had as a friend. He had even made sure I had the telephone number of his mother to keep her informed of his condition. But as I brought him a little piece of ice that night, he did not look fortunate. Surrounded by machines that made breathing and beeping noises, he writhed and stared at the ceiling and looked right through me.

"Water," he gasped again. I put a piece of ice in his mouth. He sucked on it desperately.

I sat there with him, next to the machines. No one checked on him. No one came by. It felt as though we were a hundred miles away from any other living person. It was another dark night for me, and my whole being ached.

I traveled back and forth to the nurse's station, pleading Bill's case, describing the situation. The nurse was professional but overworked. Her words were terse and firm. Each time I walked down the hall past all of the thin, silent people in beds, guarded by machines and televisions with no one sitting beside them, I thought about how many times my friend had helped me. A little bit of ice seemed pitiful compensation for the debt I owed him.

Bill and I talked that night mostly about water. To be more exact, I talked with him about water and hoped he could hear me. I put the ice to his mouth and watched his sullen eyes hanging on to the little bit of life he had left. I assured him that in the morning I would come visit him again, and we would have more time to talk about more serious things, about issues that had always interested him.

For as long as I had known him, Bill always tried to work beside me, to do anything I asked for the sake of the church. I sat and remembered how he hesitated to accept the Lord during the first few months that I knew him. Over the past few years especially, he had developed a strong sense of dignity from his relationship with Christ, and our respect for him grew deeper each time he led us in songs or helped a neighbor from getting evicted. As I held his hand to pray that night, though, his bony fingers grabbed my hand desperately. At the beginning of the prayer, he arched his back in pain, and his cracked lips mouthed desperate words. While we prayed, his body sank back into the hospital bed, and his labored breathing became more steady. He seemed to relax, if even for a moment.

I could not relax; the beeping sounds of machines, the smell of medicine, the florescent lights, and the weight of the previous dark months of my own despair and illness all seemed to compound the pain I felt as I faced the possibility of losing my friend. I tried to smile at Bill; I was, after all, still his pastor, and it was my job to try to lift his spirits in the midst of his suffering. I did not succeed at either.

"I'll come by to visit tomorrow morning, Bill," I said, encouraging him to get a good night's rest, as if that were possible for someone in the final stages of AIDS. I shook my head, feeling inadequate and empty. Again. Why did there have to be so many losses in my life? As I walked out of his room to leave, Bill whispered again to me, "More water." All I could do was pray a feeble prayer that Living Water might quench his thirst and ease his pain.

I wandered into the busy whirl of New York's night life and didn't really know how I found my way home. I just did. I was still tired, weak, and discouraged. I knew intellectually that Christ was walking with me, that he was my only hope and that Bill would be all right. But my heart felt like lead, and all I wanted to do was sleep. I honestly did not know how much longer I could keep going.

I awoke the next morning with little enthusiasm for the day. Though my body was recovering slowly from the months of sickness and internalized conflicts, it seemed as if my soul was still needing attention and care. I asked God to break through the darkness and let the dawn come. I stared at the ceiling, not really expecting anything to change. So when I walked into Bill's room later that morning, I was stunned at what I saw.

The bed was empty—neatly made and still surrounded by all the machines of the night before. Bill was gone. I froze for a minute in the vacant room. Then I swallowed and tried to regain some composure. There was a new nurse at the nurse's station.

When I asked her where Bill was, she glanced up from her work and looked me in the eyes.

"He died in the night," she said gently, looking back at her charts and continuing to work. I was numb. I looked at her for a long time. Was this the answer to my prayer? Bill was gone, and though I was thankful he wasn't suffering any longer, I wondered why God would bring him home *now,* when so much of my life already felt so fragile.

I fumbled in my pocket for a quarter and went to the pay phone in the hospital waiting room. As I pushed the coin into the telephone, I suddenly remembered Christ's promise to me that he would walk with me, that I was not alone in this. I closed my eyes in relief, thanking him for his presence beside me there in the hospital. I sighed a silent prayer of thanks and called Bill's mother.

A week later I was a part of his funeral in Brooklyn, a traditional African American funeral with Bill's entire family. It gave me more insight into who my friend was as a person, showing me a side of him I hadn't discovered while we worked together on the Lower East Side. I ached for Bill's loss but was genuinely glad he was home at last.

Fighting the Darkness

During the next few months, my body slowly regained some strength and my faith gradually rediscovered the reality of Christ's promise to walk with me. Some of the conflicts in our neighborhood and church had receded, and life was beginning to feel back to normal, at least as normal as it could be on New York's Lower East Side. But I had been here long enough to know that did not necessarily mean the battles were going to go away.

My time visiting Bill in the hospital brought back too many memories of other visits. There was the night earlier in our time at Graffiti when Mandy lurched into the storefront. I knew it wasn't going to be easy. I wasn't sure I had the energy to help her. She was one of those people we would see only sporadically throughout the years, and usually her visits meant she demanded food, clothing, or money. She was probably only about thirty years old, though she looked like she was fifty. She always wore long-sleeved shirts to hide the needle marks, and her hands were always swollen. Before the park closed, sometimes I would see her standing by some of the benches, her eyes shut, lost in a state of half-consciousness and leaning to one side. Every time she seemed about ready to tip over, she would catch herself, just enough to stay upright. I came to call this posture "the droops." From then on, whenever I saw someone standing like a statue, it usually could be associated with heroine use, and I knew that the addicts usually got their stuff from our friendly local drug dealer, Luis.

Prostitutes in our neighborhood never looked like the Hollywood version of glamorous prostitutes. Their clothes were ragged, and they were skinny, dirty, and desperate to do anything to score some drugs. Sometimes their noses were broken or their eyes swollen and black. Mandy was hardly different, and she almost always was hanging on a different guy. At least she tried more than most prostitutes to make herself look presentable.

But something was obviously wrong this Wednesday night. She held her throat and could only gasp between hard breaths: "This guy just choked me down the street. He mugged me. He pushed me against the stoop, and I can hardly breathe."

We had just finished a Bible study. "Let's get you to the hospital," I said. Lisa, another church worker, and I got into a taxi with Mandy as she continued to cough. We had never seen Mandy so restrained or subdued. She had cursed no one and demanded nothing. The back of the taxi seemed remarkably quiet compared to all the people we left shouting in the storefront. Still, I was anxious at the thought that Mandy had become a victim.

"I know God is with me in all of this," Mandy whispered to no one in particular as she wiped her mouth with a tissue. She kept coughing, and I had stared at her in the same way I later stared at the nurse the morning Bill died. Was I hearing correctly? Mandy had never talked like this. In contrast to the city noise outside, the taxi almost seemed a holy place, filled with a sense of peace. I shook my head at God's surprising presence. Mandy was not sounding like the victim of a mugging, but rather like one who knew the hope of Christ.

I sighed as the cab pulled up to the emergency room—it seemed I had been at the hospital a little too much lately. When I finally remembered I was a pastor, I took Mandy's hand and said, "I know God is with you, too, Mandy. He's promised."

We escorted Mandy through a crowded, busy emergency room. A television blared from across the room, and each row of plastic chairs was filled with all sorts of people. Some sat comatose, staring into space. Others chattered happily, as if they were in a restaurant. Many groaned in an attempt to get attention. When we finally made our way to the front desk, a family burst in behind us and nearly pushed us over.

"Oh my God, they stabbed him," the young woman screamed. "They stabbed my brother right on the street. He wasn't doing nothing. They stabbed him for nothing." She was wailing and frantic. An older woman had her arm around her and several small children tagged along, holding on to the older woman's skirt. The man's sister began to alternate between screaming and weeping. It took several people to get her to sit down and calm down.

Lisa, Mandy, and I got ready for a long wait, finding some seats across from the TV. Sometimes when we had taken people to the emergency room, we'd give them a bag lunch because we knew they might have to wait eight hours or more before they actually saw anyone. This time was different. A nurse, who looked to be about Mandy's age, apparently considered her wound pretty serious because Mandy was in an examination room after only an hour. I leaned back in my chair and closed my eyes, trying not to feel the frenzy of illness around me.

We sat in the waiting room for a long time. We tried to talk; otherwise, we'd have to hear the shouts and cries and complaints and fears of everyone in the rooms and cubicles beyond the curtain. The doctor who was examining Mandy seemed tired when he called us. He took a long time examining her throat and listening to her lungs, as if to show us the severity of her condition. Then he looked at Mandy and told her he wanted her to stay in the hospital through the night for observation.

"I can't," Mandy responded forcefully.

The doctor kept at her. "You know you have many of the symptoms of AIDS. In addition to that, you have been an IV drug user for a long time. You really need to get some treatment for this lung infection."

Mandy acted as if she hadn't heard him. "When will you be done?" she asked.

"Pretty soon," he said, glancing at us for help. "But you really need to stay in the hospital. It's really important to get some treatment."

"I need to go to the bathroom," Mandy announced and walked out to the rest room in the waiting room. "I'll just be a minute," she said, looking back at us. We followed her through the crowds, heard the door lock, and waited. Several people came up to the room, and we told them politely that it was already occupied.

After about ten minutes, though, a woman came up and pounded on the door. "Come on!" she shouted. "Get outta there! We need to get in there!" I was amazed that her loud voice could rise above the din of the emergency room, catching everyone's attention. Suddenly the entire room was quiet.

"What's wrong in there?" people began to mumble. "Is she sick, or shooting up, or what?"

"Come on!" the woman shouted even louder. "Lemme in there!"

"I'm not coming out!" We all heard Mandy's voice from inside shout.

The pounding woman then demanded the security guard come over and force Mandy from the bathroom. He strolled over as if this happened all the time and tried to act official in front of his large audience, yelling for Mandy to come out. There was no response.

"Come on, Mandy, this is enough," I finally pleaded. "Come on out and let's get things taken care of." No response.

By this time, the entire emergency room was in an uproar, incensed that this woman had taken their only bathroom. The room of people began to boil, and I was nervous when it felt like the beginning of a riot. The guard tried to control the crowd, but they kept yelling.

When the doctor heard the commotion, he came out into the waiting room. I went over to him to ask if there was anything specific we needed to do to help her.

"She's got to get treatment," the doctor told me, flipping through some charts. "She shouldn't be on the street. She may be infecting a lot of other people." Just as he said this to me, Mandy shot out of the rest room and ran into the street. I ran outside to find her, but the street was so crowded I had no idea in what direction she had gone.

We looked for an hour but never found her. People brushed past me in the eerie night, asking for change or a drink or some sort of help. I had had enough. It was now about four o'clock in the morning, and I couldn't bear the thought of talking with one more person. I took a long way home so I wouldn't have to see any of the night people I knew. My strategy didn't exactly work, and I ran into a young dope addict I had met at the park once. Rocko was playing his guitar. He was high and talkative.

"Hey, listen to the song I just wrote. Hey, wait a minute. Stop; just listen."

I kept walking. "I just can't listen right now, Rocko. I'll have to hear it tomorrow." I kept moving one foot in front of the other. I wondered where Mandy was.

Rocko followed me. His eyes narrowed, and then he hurled a barrage of words at me like they were rocks: "You call yourself a Christian? You're a nothing. You're a zero. You won't even stop to listen to my song. I hope you rot in hell!"

I put my hand on my head as if to protect myself. "You're right, Rocko," I said as I kept trying to walk. "I'm a nothing. A zero." When I finally arrived home, I collapsed in my bed and didn't wake up until late the next afternoon.

Three days later I was walking to the church and noticed Mandy standing on the corner. Her head wagged back and forth; her eyes darted up and down the street. She shifted her weight as she talked with a man I hadn't seen before. She saw me coming, and told him to go buy some cigarettes for her. He did.

I approached her like an old friend. "Mandy, it sounds as though you have AIDS. You've got to take care of yourself. You could be giving AIDS to a lot of other people," I said quietly.

Mandy looked at me as if I were an idiot. "I don't have AIDS," she proclaimed. Her hands shook, and at that moment I could tell the darkness had beaten her. I tried to help, but nothing would get through. Then, without saying another word to me, Mandy walked across the street to join the guy who had bought her cigarettes. She glanced back at me, walked into the busy crowd with her "friend," and disappeared.

I saw her only a few times after that, and she never did talk with me again. I cringe to think of how she must have suffered. About a year later, someone told me she had died, probably of an overdose. We held a memorial service for Mandy in Graffiti's storefront, and I pleaded with the friends who had gathered to remember how Christ would rather carry our pain then have us numb it with drugs or other temporary relief. We had seen too many friends die of AIDS or drug-related incidents. Only Christ was able to take our burdens and give us the peace we longed for.

It was a message that would come back to me each time I'd remember losing a friend to AIDS. I wondered when the dawn would begin to break.

Losing Luis

By June, my body was nearly fully recovered from months of fatigue and sickness. I was trying to take life one day at a time, and my soul was encouraged to find God waiting for me each morning. The Scriptures were coming alive to me again, and my heart was starting to sing a little more each time I walked through the neighborhood and into Graffiti. Of course I knew life on the Lower East Side was not suddenly void of the problems that had long marked it; drugs and homelessness, illiteracy and unemployment had not gone away overnight just because my spiritual vision was back on track. The difference for me now was that I knew I did not have to fight the battles and tensions of these issues alone. No, my job—as Jesus had been gracious to remind me—was simply to give him my burdens and to be faithful in what he had called me to do.

I went more slowly as I returned to work. One particular morning, I walked through the neighborhood, picked up a cup of coffee from a local deli, and strolled past a group of women sitting on the front stoop of a familiar apartment building. I stopped to chat with these neighbors as they sat together in the morning sun, and I noticed their attitude seemed different. Their faces looked almost shell-shocked. I asked them if they were all right.

"They got them all last night, Pastor," one of the women said in a lifeless voice as she turned her head toward me. I was confused. "At least fifty federal agents came in and picked them all up. They got Luis, and they got my daughter's husband too. I don't know what she's going to do, with the new baby and all."
It took me a second to comprehend what I had just heard. Luis, the main supplier of heroine and crack and dope in our neighborhood, had been arrested? The short little man-of-steel whom

no one ever messed with around here had met his match? Was it true that the thoughtful karate instructor and drug dealer who kept waiting to give his life to God was now in jail? Maybe things really were beginning to change.

I sipped my coffee and listened some more, startled by both the news of Luis's arrest and the concern of these friends. Emotions were flying. Another woman blurted out, "God will judge whoever squealed on them. They had no right to come into this neighborhood and do that." The others agreed. I asked them if they really thought the arrest was a bad thing. Again, words and opinions flew around the street like a blizzard in January.

"You'll see, Pastor. This neighborhood's going to be hurt by what happened. Children will suffer because the money's gone. You'll see." I listened without responding. Some of these same women were volunteers at Graffiti, and I realized this was indeed going to present a serious economic issue for these families.

I tried to encourage them, but my words offered little help in the midst of what they perceived as a major tragedy. As the group sat on the stoop and stared blankly at the buildings across the street, fear spread across their faces.

I went back to the deli, bought a newspaper, and turned the pages until I found the small article about how federal drug enforcement agents had broken up a long-standing operation on the Lower East Side, finally capturing a notorious drug king. The paper called him "The King of Seventh Street." I glanced up and shook my head. First the park closing, then pneumonia, now this. What was God doing? The man who had seemed invincible had finally been arrested, and now the neighborhood was in shock. He was the man whom everyone looked up to. He was the one many families went to when they were in trouble. What would happen now?

"You watch," another neighbor told me as I walked back up the street toward Graffiti. "There's going to be a lot more trouble here now. Things will get stolen; cars will get broken into." I told him I had my doubts. He tried to convince me. "Man, those guys protected the whole neighborhood. They didn't want this street to attract any attention. This block's going downhill."

Neighbors were right about one thing: the street was definitely different, especially at night. There were no more lookouts, none of Luis's men hurrying people along or telling them they couldn't come down this street. There were no more intense interactions in the middle of the block between junkies and suppliers. True, the kids would not have their karate lessons anymore, but they also wouldn't have to dodge heroine addicts wandering up and down the block, desperate for a fix.

Apparently, the federal agents had observed Luis for a long time, probably long before the park had closed. They had compiled enough evidence and enough witnesses to take Luis and many of his men off the street and into jail. At his trial, he decided to plead guilty in exchange for some plea bargains, considering the extensive case against him. Luis was sentenced to over fifteen years in prison.

My reaction to his loss was bittersweet. Though I always hated what he did—how the crack and heroine he supplied destroyed the lives of people like Mandy and countless others— I nonetheless liked the person of Luis. I couldn't help but respect the fact that he cared about children and about helping out his neighbors, even if it was with mixed motives. I wasn't sure if I'd ever see Luis again, but I did feel confident that his arrest was part of God's intervention in the life of our community. And if my resolve had been shaky before and after the park closed, it was solidified now that the block around our church was free of this drug operation. Yes, Luis's arrest did present many financial hardships to local families, but it also opened many more doors for us to offer hope and help to our neighbors in the love of Jesus. I felt things were looking up.

I had to confess, though, I was shocked a couple of weeks after his arrest when I went to the mailbox and found a letter from this same man, the one who had once been called the most respected man in the neighborhood. I turned it over in my hand, almost afraid to open it.

"Dear Pastor, Well, I have finally done what we talked about." I read the letter slowly, not fully believing what I was seeing. "I have accepted the Lord and become a Christian. Please come to visit me. I have many things to talk to you about. Can you baptize me? —Luis."

Yes, the dawn had broken.

"Thank you, Jesus!" I exclaimed. I could hardly wait to pass on the news to our congregation. I was sure Luis's decision would encourage many of our people; first, though, I needed to visit him myself.

It took some time, but I was finally cleared to visit in the federal prison that sat just a few miles south of the Lower East Side. It was likely Luis would eventually be moved from this facility, but at least for now I could visit him by simply getting on a subway. I entered the prison somewhat nervous, but eager to see Luis. Prison guards searched me and then led me into a glass room about the size of a closet. The small glass rooms were next to a larger waiting room, where prisoners sat with their families and talked. I watched children running up and down long rows of chairs.

Then Luis was brought in, walking straight and tall. I swallowed. But almost instantly, I noticed something different about him. He did not appear to be as tough as he had been when I saw him on our block. His shoulders shook a bit, and his eyes were softer than I had ever seen them. When he sat down, he began to weep. Once again God's presence surprised me, but I knew this man had come to the end of himself. He had let go of trying to control his own life and was now broken because of it.

"Everything's changed for me now," he said, wiping his eyes. "I'm not saying it's been easy. It's been terrible. But God hasn't let me go." I listened as Luis confessed to me how worried he was for his family and how difficult it had been for him being in prison. Officials had placed a "no move" order on him here because of some of the other inmates. That meant Luis was not allowed to go to chapel, church services, or Bible study. He had been discouraged—until they moved him to a new floor.

"I was standing next to a guy I didn't know up there on the new floor, a guy who used 'God' a lot in his talk. So I asked if he was a Christian, and he said he was. I told him I was too. He said he had a surprise for me the next day." I hoped it wouldn't be a bad dream. Luis continued: "The next day when we got together, that guy told me to follow him. I saw another guy come out of the cell at the end of the hall, grinning at me. Things had been pretty weird, so I thought maybe this was a set-up. As we came to the cell, I could see about fifteen guys in the room, about three on each bunk, and I just knew they were going to jump me. Then I figured it'd happen sooner or later, so I walked into the cell anyway."

I knew Luis was not easily intimidated, that his anger could be explosive. But never had I seen him so open. I pulled my chair in closer, knowing the former drug king was actually afraid. He finished his story.

"Then the biggest guy stood up and looked me in the eyes. And you know what he did? He reached his arms out, gave me a hug, and said, *'Dios te bendiga'*—God be with you. Then they told me they met on their own every day, not under the supervision of the Chapel. They just met to encourage each other." Luis relaxed a bit and looked straight at me, just like he had that night I had told him we would not take his money for a block party.

"They let me know that God hasn't forgotten me. Course, sometimes I just want to fight the devil, and I ask God to let me take him on. But then God teaches me, step by step, what I ought to do instead. You need to pray for me." So we bowed our heads in the prison waiting room, and I asked God to protect Luis during his time in prison and to be near him, especially during difficult situations. It was a sight that earlier I would not have had faith to believe was possible: a famous Hispanic drug king praying with the skinny, anglo minister from the block he once ruled. But it was the second time I realized how much I had in common with Luis: we both had called on Jesus to pull us out of a dark and difficult time. He had heard our prayers.

When I got home, the people in the church decided to write Luis a card. I glanced at what Eli, one of our first teenagers to be baptized, wrote: "I used to look up to you for all the wrong reasons. But now that you've come to the Lord, I look up to you for all the right reasons." A new day had come at last.

*Adventures tend to
make you late for dinner.*
—J. R. R. TOLKEIN
THE LORD OF THE RINGS

chapter ten
A Place Called Home

There is nothing like stepping out of a dark dingy cellar and into fresh sunlight. That is how it felt for me when Christ broke through the darkness of my difficult months and took the burdens I had internalized for too long. It was like my lungs were full again of fresh air, and I realized that many of the previous circumstances and events—particularly Luis's arrest and conversion—marked a milestone for both our work and my health. I was eager to start again.

With new eyes, I began working again at Graffiti with more energy and focus; my strength continued to return. As I walked the familiar route through the neighborhood and into the office, my step now seemed lighter than it had before. Though the buildings and faces I passed hadn't changed much, something felt different for me, almost as if my soul was more carefree than it had been in years. For the first time in a long time, it felt refreshing—not draining—to be back at Graffiti. Especially one Monday morning as I opened the door to our office and noticed a sign on the bulletin board that hung over the main entrance:

A small, nonpoisonous baby python was lost in the Graffiti storefront last Wednesday night. If you see the snake, please contain it and contact us immediately. Thank you.

I smiled, knowing once again I was in the right place.

Singing Again

"What happened?" I asked Mary, who, along with some faithful volunteers, had been keeping everything together at the mission while I was getting well. I set down my briefcase and settled into my chair, glancing around the familiar room. I loved this place.

Mary took a sip of her coffee as she relayed the story to me: "Last Wednesday at the Bible study, one of the guys brought his snake in his pocket, even though I'd told him not to. The Bible study went fine until the end when Eli asked the guy if he could see the snake. He checked his pocket, but it was gone."

I tried to make sense of what she just described. Then again, it wasn't hard to imagine something like this at *our* Bible study.

"You mean it crawled out of his pocket *during* the Bible study?" I asked, trying to get it right.

She nodded, looking around at the room's floor, as if she were searching for something. I followed Mary's eyes, wondering how no one could have noticed a slithering black snake crawl from a man's pocket. It must have been some Bible study!

Mary continued, still looking: "We spent the night and the next day trying to find it. The snake specialist said it would probably eat rodents, grow bigger, and come out much later."

I shrugged my shoulders and said, "Well, that's something to look forward to." We both laughed. We knew that if Graffiti was about anything, it was about ongoing adventures like baby snakes at Bible studies. It was about discovering the things we never expected to find and losing those things we always thought we'd keep.

I was sure this would be an adventurous week. I dove into days full of my usual pastoral duties—meeting with people, returning phone calls, and overseeing our programs at four different sites around the neighborhood. My heart was singing again, and I was glad to be a part of God's unique work here.

But by Wednesday night I had to admit I was a little concerned that we still had not discovered the little python anywhere in our building. This week I was able to join the volunteer Bible teacher from our mother church for what was likely to be another lively discussion of Scripture.

As I walked into the small room where we met, I saw Skippy already arranging the chairs. I patted him on the back and asked how he was doing. Skippy was living on the sidewalk at the time and liked to sing songs about his mental illness. "Just fine," he said, moving the chairs.

I glanced every now and then at the floor just in case I saw anything move. Before long, others strolled in from the street and took their seats. I talked with a few, looked around the room, and enjoyed watching the familiar faces of these friends. Amazingly, I did not hear one person mention the snake. What I did hear was Skippy suddenly break into one of his short terse tunes.

"The best thing . . . about . . . losing it . . .," he thundered philosophically, as if he were in a Broadway musical, "is . . . that you don't have to . . . *carry* . . . it with you!" His timing was impeccable. He gave me a knowing grin, rubbed his beard, and winked at me as if we shared a secret. I was inspired.

"OK, let's get everybody together to sing a song!" I announced. And sing we did. For at least ten minutes, we made it through a couple of choruses and hymns, singing as loud as we could. Victor, with long silver hair, began to dance. Another man fell asleep. A lady began to beat time with her cane. Skippy put his head in his hands. It was just like the old days.

When we finished singing, I glanced at the floor and then to the faces of the ten or so people who had gathered. "Now we are going to have our meditation time," I continued.

"Medication time!" someone shouted, and we all burst into laughter. Lori, the cook, played some more music on the electric piano. Skippy began to sigh deeply. I sat back in my chair, glancing a few times at the feet in the circle in case a baby python wanted to make an appearance at any moment.

"We're going to continue talking about the tough time Paul had in 2 Corinthians," the Bible teacher announced. *Good choice,* I thought, as I quietly cheered him on.

"Paul ain't the only one with sufferin'," said Annabel, the woman with crutches who had previously kicked her doctor. All of our heads turned to her as she demanded, "Look at me! My eyes need an operation. My lock don't work, and my legs don't work either." The Bible study teacher shuffled a bit in his chair, trying unsuccessfully to regain control. The woman was going to be heard.

"I'm fed up, and do you know what happened this week?" she asked us, her eyes bouncing from one face to the next. She did not wait for an answer. "I had to go to the emergency room because of a problem in my head. Do you know what it was?" We could only imagine, but again we did not have time to respond.

"It was a roach in my ear." She paused to let her words sink in. My eyes shot to the floor, but again it was empty. She went on: "The doctor said in his twenty-five years of practice, he hadn't ever seen anything like it. So, what I want to know is, why do I have so much sufferin'?" Murmurs of sincere sympathy arose from the group. I flipped through my Bible like it was a fan. Skippy brought his face up, and then put it back down into his hands to show his remorse.

The Bible teacher hesitated and then took charge again. "I know we've talked about suffering a lot. I don't know why all these terrible things are happening to you," he held his gaze as he tried to reassure the woman. "I have to admit that some of the things you share are things I have never heard before. But I do know that Jesus is taking these terrible things and bringing good out of them. You are being glorified through your sufferings." He offered her a patient smile. But the woman slammed her crutches on the ground.

"Then would you please tell Jesus," she pronounced each word fiercely, "to stop glorifyin' me!"

The room erupted into shouts and laughter and counter-arguments. After about twenty minutes of chaotic discussion about Paul and roaches and suffering and Jesus, I announced we were going to have a closing prayer. I stood up and thanked God for letting us be together again and for the truth that Jesus wants to take our sufferings for us. After a roomful of hearty amens, Skippy and the others put back the chairs and wandered out into the street, helping the woman with crutches. It felt good again to be at Bible study.

As I was locking the door to leave, I looked once again across the floor and again saw nothing. That snake didn't slither into the light during our Bible study that night. Or the next week either for that matter. Or the next. But Bible studies were plenty interesting without it. And for all I know, it's still "growing" somewhere in the building, a little reminder that no one ever quite knows what adventures are going to emerge in urban ministry.

Brave Youth

Thursday nights our youth gathered for Bible study and fun. It had been a while since I had seen some of these young people, so I decided to join them the next night to catch up. Teenagers with big baggy jeans and long T-shirts shuffled into the room; they wore baseball caps and high-top sneakers, some even carried Bibles, a very uncool thing to do a few years ago but now—especially since Luis accepted Christ—it was more than acceptable. Eli, Jose, Carlos, and about a dozen others sat in a circle laughing and talking as if they didn't have a care in the world. I knew, of course, that they did, that daily they felt the pressures of living in a neighborhood where the drug culture was prominent. On this block, grandmothers told their children to sell dope because they could make more money than if they worked at McDonald's. Most of their friends thought school was a joke, and few graduated from high school. These kids at Graffiti, I knew, felt the odds against them every day. Maybe that's why they came to our youth group at all; this place at least was relatively safe, and they knew the people here were for them, not against them. After years of working primarily with the homeless on the Lower East Side, God had given us more and more opportunities to reach out to the next generation through our youth groups, children's ministry, and summer camp programs. They were the future of our ministry, and I was proud of these young people.

Tonight, I found myself looking at the faces of these teenagers in a new way, grateful for the fact that they were here at all. I wondered what life had in store for some of them, and I remembered what many had gone through to get here. When I noticed Jose's face, I couldn't help but ask him if he remembered the time he had run away from his mother, which was one of my first "initiations" into the neighborhood. Shortly after I had arrived at Graffiti, his mother had come up to me frantic that her son was gone.

"Jose has run away. He's only fourteen years old," she said to me outside the church, panic and fear in her voice. "He can't take care of himself, and he's probably gone to Coney Island. I'm going to the precinct to report him."

I told her I'd see if I could find out anything from the other kids, so I began to walk down the street. A man who must have overheard us on the sidewalk grabbed my elbow, looked around suspiciously, and whispered to me, "I think Jose's in that building over there." He pointed across an empty lot to a dark abandoned building a block away, and then he disappeared into the blur of the night. I wasn't too excited about walking into an abandoned building with friends during the day, much less alone at night, but I had told Jose's mother I'd help.

The building was seven stories high, with broken, blackened windows looming above me in the streetlight like some Gothic masterpiece.

"I know you're here, God," I said as I pushed on the metal door, hoping it would be locked. Instead, it gave a little as I pushed, and I stepped through the entrance. Inside was complete blackness.

"Anybody here?" I blurted into the darkness. No answer. I heard some people moving around on the floors above, but no answer. "Is Jose here?" I shouted, my voice quivering. No answer.

With my hand on the hallway wall, I started walking deeper into the building. *I'm going to step on a junkie,* I thought. *Someone's going to stab me, and no one will ever find me. What am I doing here?* Something rustled close to my feet. Adrenaline rushed through my skin like a subway train. *Just a rat,* I thought.

I was deep in the building now, and it was like being in a cave. No lights. Something dripping somewhere. People scurrying around upstairs, but not talking. Maybe they are trying to get away from me. Or maybe they're getting ready to attack me. I pressed my hand earnestly to the moist wall and prayed again.

Someone came bustling toward me from the back of the building. He was carrying something in his hands, perhaps some boards. I could hear the boards hitting the walls as he walked through the rooms.

"I'm looking for Jose!" I shouted, trying to sound normal as I stood in the pitch darkness. "Have you seen him?"

"Yeah!" the voice said. I still couldn't see a thing, but I knew he was inches away. His voice sounded routine, not like someone who was going to stab me. Talking to someone in total darkness in the middle of an abandoned building late at night seemed normal to him. "I think Jose's upstairs. On the third floor. The stairs are right in front of you."

"OK." I tried to sound normal, too, as if this were the usual way I made pastoral visits. I found the banister and started towards the second story of this ramshackle building, walking in the darkness. I climbed higher and higher, following the banister as the stairs turned. I felt as though I had climbed about thirty feet when the man downstairs suddenly called to me in his casual tone. By this time my heart was pounding in my frame like a sledgehammer.

"Hey, wait a minute!" he shouted. "You need a light. There are some stairs missing up there." Then he jumped the steps, two at a time in total darkness, to where I was; placed in my hand a matchbox with several matches in it; and bounced back down the stairs to do his work. I lit one.

For the first time I could see the gray, dirty walls and the crumbling makeshift stairway. Terror gripped me as I looked ahead—the next four steps were gone! If I had taken another step, I would have dropped into that gaping black mouth and gone straight down. I couldn't see how far the drop would be, but it sounded substantial as plaster and wood chips spilled over the edge. Now my fear of the darkness was replaced by the reality that I had almost dropped to my death looking for Jose. I caught my breath before I was able to take a few more steps.

On the second floor, some light from the street shone through a broken window, and I was able to find my way to the third floor. "Is Jose here?" I asked a group of teenagers huddled against a wall, trying to sound casual.

"Naw," they said. "He left a long time ago." I sighed.

"Do you know where he went?"

"Maybe Coney Island. Who knows?"

I retraced my steps, remembering the four missing stairs, and left much more quickly than I had entered. I went back to our storefront, exhausted, still wondering what I was doing here. As I waited for news from Jose's mother, I looked through the mail on my desk. There was a letter in a child's handwriting from a Sunday school class in the suburbs. I knew I needed some encouragement. I opened it.

"Dear Missionary," it said, scrawled out in third-grade writing. "I am praying for you and all the other people on drugs." This choice of grammar had included me in a new way. I thanked God for children's prayers, and prayed for more missions education.

When I ran into Jose the next day, he acted as if nothing had happened.

"That's because I was just wackin' out." The now-older Jose interrupted my memory as we shared the rest of the story at Thursday night youth group. This was a kid whose father probably drank himself to death, a kid who was trying to make sense of street life when he first started coming to Graffiti. After he became a Christian, he was one of our first local youth hired by the North American Mission Board summer employment program (called Sojourners) to work in the community. Jose worked as a camp counselor for Sojourners; he even went on to graduate from high school and get a nondrug-related job—a first for his family. It was exciting to hear how far he had come as he explained what happened.

"Man, I was so messed up then. I felt like the 'Christian' thing was messin' with me, too, 'cause no one understood then what I was doing. They made fun of me, how I accepted Christ and everything. Like I was somebody from outer space. I just left that night to get away for a while."

When they heard him say this, the other teens joined Jose in the discussion of how tough it had been to be a Christian in our neighborhood in those days. Then Carlos chimed in. I reminded him how he had surprised me the day he told me about his conversion one Sunday after church. He had come forward during the invitation and asked to be baptized, even though he was one of the toughest guys around—black hair down to his shoulders, hip-hop-style boxers, and low-riding pants. Carlos never said much; he only grunted his answers.

When I had asked him if he had asked Christ into his life that Sunday morning, he shook his head no. I pressed him, wondering if it had been on the youth trip to camp in Kentucky a few weeks before. Again, he shook his head no. "Then when did you come to Christ?" I asked the then-thirteen-year-old. He pushed his hair back and grunted, "Three years ago when Mary [our children's director] was telling us that Bible story." I was amazed. Three more times I asked him, and three more times he told me he accepted Christ when Mary had told them a specific Bible story.

I prayed with Carlos that day, made arrangements for his baptism to take place at our mother church in a few weeks, and went looking for Mary. This blonde single woman from Alabama had been our children's director for a while, starting with about twenty kids and now interacting with more than five hundred children, directing all the sites and activities. She had seen a lot of tough kids come and go, and she knew the challenges that faced them. So I was surprised as anyone when she started to cry after I told her what Carlos had said.

"He was the boy who almost made me leave the first week I got here," she whispered. Then she told me how she had been telling a Bible story to this group of kids one day at boys' club. Carlos was there with his younger brother, and apparently, his brother was not exactly interested in church. When he asked why they had to "listen to this stupid story," Carlos turned to him, punched him as hard as he could in the nose, and watched the blood splatter all over the floor in Mary's classroom. Then Carlos merely answered his brother, "'Cause Jesus loves us, stupid."

We laughed about it now as we retold the story of his somewhat forceful evangelism method. Then we turned to listen to Eli. Everyone respected Eli. When I first met him on our block, he was a twelve-year-old chubby kid with an Afro. Within months of attending our programs, Eli asked Christ into his heart, knowing it was not going to be easy for him to be a Christian in this neighborhood. Two of his friends even came to his baptism just to make fun of him. Instead, they ended up asking him questions afterward. When I listened to how he answered them, I knew early on that Eli was a special young man.

"Yeah, I got Christ in my heart, and I'm forgiven for my sins," he told them. "Man, this is the thing I just gotta do. You do too." Apparently, it made sense to them, too, so together we prayed, and they received Christ into their hearts. I hugged them, told their parents, and invited them to keep coming to the program. Two years later, when one of Eli's young converts died of an asthma attack, Eli knew he had done the right thing to share with him.

But it never got easier for Eli. Though he started writing Christian rap and working for us in the Sojourners program, it wasn't long before his mother died after a long illness. I had visited her in the hospital and knew she didn't have much more time left. When she passed away, Eli had to go live with his grandmother twenty blocks away. That was like moving to another state for us; we thought we'd never see him again.

The next week at youth group, however, Eli walked in. He was there the following week as well. He became involved with our Graffiti Partnership program and developed a friendship with an adult mentor, a young professional businessman in advertising named Steve. Steve took Eli to his office, on commercial shoots, and to dinner. Eli loved seeing more of the city with Steve and became more and more responsive to his direction. Though he was continually pressured by his community to join the drug culture, where he could easily have made thousands a week, Eli chose to work for us instead. His peers never stopped making fun of him for being a Christian, but I often heard him say to them, "There's no pension plan for a drug dealer; you either die or go to jail."

Despite the pressure, Eli never quit. He became one of the few young men to graduate from high school. Then, largely through Steve and Mary's help, Eli entered college to study communication and mass media, one of the first teens on the block to go to college. Summer after summer he still comes back to help lead our children's programs. In fact, Eli has now become the most respected man in the neighborhood, taking kids under his wing and reminding them in his gentle way about Christ's love.

Because of all he has gone through, I consider Eli to be the bravest man I know. He could have taken a turn into the streets, but he continually made the choice to walk the harder road as a Christian. We sat quietly talking with the group that night of my return, reflecting on how much God had worked in all of our lives. Then someone asked Eli for his now-famous Graffiti rap, one that has since been made into a video with Eli in the starring role. He obliged, stood up, and "preached" a message all the teens could relate to:

"We Pray Hard"

by Eli De Jesus

(Refrain) *When I say* Jesus, *you say* Christ

Jesus	Christ
Jesus	Christ

When I say Gave His, *you say* Life

Gave His	Life
Gave His	Life

From the lower deck
With Tompkins type 'X'
You look at somebody wrong
You might catch wreck
I don't know why
Maybe it's the stress
or the crime
and drugs
and sees the rest
But since about 10 years old I been down with the clique
of the Jick, click
Graffiti I pick
Not the art, but the church I say
To help me through my weakest times
and my saddest days
Like when my mom she passed
Times was rough
I was buggin, flippin
Enough was enough
Time to chill, stay in school and
Keep it real
Cause I wasn't tryin to

heave ya' fallin' off kid
Yo! I'm too nice for that
I'm gonna make it big with God by my side
And all through my life
I stab the devil with my spiritual knife
and only G O D could be the king for me
And if G O D be in me, then the king I be
(repeat the last two lines)
(Refrain)

Yo, When I pray to God
I pray from the heart
My words come out like a form of art
I say what I say 'cause I know he cares
I say what I say 'cause I know he's there
To help me through the good
To help me through the bad
There was one period of time I was very, very sad
My mom just passed
I had no clue what to do
How would I get through?
What would you do?
Hey, yo, Mess up in school?
Be a little fool?
I said, "no!" 'Cause I ain't goin' out like that!
(repeat)
My mom raised me better than a stubborn little brat
and that's like Big Bird
I will live my life right
in spite of all the evil I see in the night.

So, I take care
Stop! Look! Don't Stare!
Cause the world's not fair
So I say a prayer

And do what I gotta do
With God I grew
And I stay true
Why?
Cause I owe it to the crew
And I pray hard.
(refrain)

Applause and cheers went up for Eli as we finished our youth group meeting for the night. I watched the teens shuffle back into the street and toward home—baggy jeans and Bibles—knowing, in fact, that some of the young people in our Lower East Side neighborhood *did* pray hard. Life is not easy for them, though it's no secret that Luis's arrest was also a turning point for many of these teenagers. Before his arrest, only a few—like Eli, Carlos, and Jose—had come to Christ. Since then, thirty to forty more teens have entered into a life-changing relationship with Jesus. Thankfully, it's become almost cool to be a Christian in our neighborhood.

No Place Like Home

A few months after hearing Eli's inspiring rap again, I was on a plane to Virginia. I'd been asked to speak at a Baptist church there about urban mission and inner city work. As a North American Mission Board sponsored missionary, I'm often invited to come and talk about inner city ministries at churches, to give people a picture of what Graffiti is about, and to express our gratitude for NAMB's support. But I have to confess: it's always a little disorienting for me because speaking in suburban or rural churches about New York's Lower East Side feels a little like going from one planet to another. Compared to what I'm used to seeing each day, I feel as if I'm entering an entirely different adventure with a different tenor. Even so, I consider it one of the many ways God is reconciling his people.

This particular Sunday morning I was wearing a pastor's robe and standing behind a huge pulpit with an elaborate sound system. Hundreds of well-dressed families sat on cushioned pews in a beautiful sanctuary under magnificent stained glass windows. Everyone was clean. Everyone had nice teeth. Everyone was polite.

As I began telling them stories about Graffiti Ministries, I noticed many of the members nodding at me with kind, benevolent faces, smiling and affirming our "difficult" work with streetwise youth and homeless men and women. I told them the story of Eli, a brave young Christian man from our neighborhood who now attended college and was serving as a much-needed role model to our children; of Bill, my good friend and music leader who died last year of AIDS; of Peggy, a woman who overcame her addiction to accumulating junk and moved into a quiet senior citizen's apartment; and finally, of Luis, a once-prominent drug dealer who now wrote me letters each month from prison telling me the latest lesson he was learning through his relationship with Christ. A few people shifted in their pews; in the second row, one man wearing a dark print tie yawned. A few immaculately coiffed ladies smiled and kept nodding; they seemed sincerely interested in Graffiti. I continued.

"Paul's letter to the Ephesians says that God's plan is to reconcile all things through Christ," I read the Scripture, a little surprised to hear my voice reverberate throughout the sanctuary.
Lights hung from the high ceiling, strong and hot. A few people
flipped through their Bibles.

"In this letter, the church is a pilot project for what God
wants to do. I believe God uses the church, with all its weakness, as the graduate school for the principalities and powers."
I noticed one of the ushers, wearing a three-piece suit, look at
his watch.

"Our weakness is really the envelope for God's power," I said,
recalling some of the times God had taught me this through the
years. There was Jacob with his family of dogs, who wanted me
to help him bury his favorite pup; George, the "priest," who had
lived in an abandoned building but who now owns his own
home in another state; Tommy, who sat beside me in his wheelchair as the park was closed, rededicated his life to Christ, and
sadly, died a few years ago of an asthma attack. I told them the
miracle of LaGuardia's recovery from alcoholism when she
came to Christ, how her husband Mike became a Christian as a
result and learned to read, but how we lost LaGuardia last year
to a stroke. I told them that sometimes our weakness seems to
win over God's power; Mike was devastated by his wife's death,
went back to drinking after that, and we never saw him again.
But all these stories, I said to the congregation that Sunday
morning, had been examples to me of how God works through
weakness, how he becomes personally involved in the broken
individual lives of people like you and me. I paused. Then I said
something about Christ's love as I stared out at the neat, orderly
congregation, at the kind, nodding faces, and suddenly felt . . .
homesick.

As I sat down, the polished pipe organ began to play. Everyone stood up like a vast army and sang in four-part harmony, "A Mighty Fortress Is Our God." We sang every verse perfectly; the ushers passed brass collection plates, and the pastor entered the pulpit to close the service with an eloquent prayer. Then he turned toward me as the congregation was dismissed.

"Thank you so much for coming, Taylor," he said, shaking my hand. He spoke with confidence; he stood erect. His shirt was crisp and white, and there was no doubt in anyone's mind that he was a natural leader. I nodded.

Within an hour, I was on a plane back to New York City. I took a bus from LaGuardia Airport to midtown Manhattan and caught a subway to the Lower East Side. I took off my tie, changed into tennis shoes, and walked along Seventh Street where the mission storefront is, hoping to make the ending of our worship service there. I noticed the neighborhood was actually changing a little. Some of the abandoned buildings had been pulled down or were being renovated into condominiums. There were no lookouts on the corner, no drug deals going on in the middle of the block, no one living in Tompkins Square Park. I had received several letters from Luis recently, who was having a tough time, and wanted to write him back about all that was happening.

I turned the corner and realized the kids and the youth and even the adults were finding new heroes. But for every good thing that had happened to someone in our neighborhood, I also knew there was great sadness. Yes, the neighborhood was being rebuilt, but low-income people were also being pushed out. Some people had achieved great victories; others had fallen. It felt bittersweet. I was eager to get to the storefront.

When I pushed open the door, the smell of many people in unwashed clothes hit me in the face. Service was just letting out. Skippy, who knew he had "lost it all," was hugging Big Jane, who had her dog with her. Lori, the cook, was still playing the little electric piano. Sam, who used to carry the butcher knife, was laughing way too loudly and slapping Andy on the back. Sam had prayed to accept the Lord, but he was still working on "trust issues." Andy, who had thrown his Bible like a missile, was smiling at the volunteer Bible study teacher. Mary and Lisa were tickling two giggling little girls. Victor, with long white hair, was dancing around with a cup of coffee, splashing most of it on the floor. My wife, Susan, and our two teen-age sons were talking with their friends.

This church called Graffiti, this family of ordinary people, this place called home, is one I could never imagine leaving. I made my way through the small crowd and grabbed a cup of water; Susan saw me, hurried over, hugged me, and asked me how my trip was. All I could think to tell her was, "I'm home!" I shouted above the laughter and chaos of our friends and received a few waves, grins, and "heys" before the buzz of the room returned to normal. And we stood talking for a long time.

> *Because I have a thorn in my foot,*
> *I can jump higher than those with sound feet.*
> —SOREN KIERKEGAARD

epilogue
Loser-Friendly Christianity

I remember hearing a preacher talk once about an intense word study he was involved in concerning the word *Hallelujah!* Of course, literally we know *Hallelujah* means "praise God," but this man wanted to find a true equivalent in our own language and culture. After great pains and much research, he boiled down all his studies to this one solitary phrase: "Hot dog, this is it!"

So, we at Graffiti began borrowing his contemporary phrase. No matter how hard or depressing the day turned, we would try to find one good thing that happened and shout, "Hot dog, this is it!" As we saw the number of victories begin to outnumber the defeats, we would cheer, "Hot dog, this is it!" We even began to shout it in the middle of church services. Sometimes Victor, who spoke mostly Spanish, stood up in the middle of my sermon and shouted, "Hallelujah, this is a hot dog!" The words weren't exactly right, but we all knew what he meant.

Today, as I walk through the streets of our neighborhood, I know there is a real battle still going on. Thankfully, there have been some hard-won victories, but there have also been real casualties. There have been many dreams conquered, but there have also been many lives shattered. There is no denying it. Yet, even with so much difficulty, I can't help but walk with a spring in my step. And on most days, I really do hear myself saying, "Hot dog, this is it!"

Why? I suppose it's because I'm realizing that the *it* at the end of our hot dog exclamation really is a brilliant and enormous Kingdom that does not fit neatly into my traditional Christian categories. My former systems of organizing and theologizing, I see now, are merely "broken lights" to God. Our attempts to explain all that God has in mind for us is a little like having a baby rat on the Lower East Side attempt to understand the coastline of Florida—and then communicate it to you. God's kingdom is a *big* kingdom!

After fifteen years of urban ministry, I have begun to believe—really believe—that God is the only one who can do far more than we can ever ask or imagine (Eph. 3:20). Sure, I can imagine a lot of things in New York City. For instance, I can imagine well-dressed professionals on Wall Street sitting down and talking with people who have no place to lay their heads for the night. I can imagine groups of individuals who happen to believe that God's strength is made perfect in weakness and meeting in the parks and tenement buildings of our toughest streets to sit down and encourage one another. I can imagine drug dealers, child abusers, overzealous realtors, high-rent gen-Xers, and angry anarchists with their arms around each other and the stunned look of repentance on their faces.

I can imagine these things because I have watched God make them happen.

I can also imagine a place where every child, teenager, and adult can read, where every inner-city young person has the same opportunities his friends in the suburbs have. I can imagine a truly rebuilt city, not just bricks and mortar, but one where people's hearts have been rebuilt and knit together through Christ's terrible tenderness. I can imagine groups of people on every floor of the housing projects gathering together—excited to worship Christ, read his Word, and pray for one another. I can imagine spontaneous praise—people in thousands of apartments lifting their windows and praising God as loudly as they can, some even yelling, "Hot dog, this is it!" I can imagine a revival of sorts, where no one says, "Look what this church did" or "Look what this person did," but where everyone says, "Look what God has done!"

I can imagine a lot of things. But God can do far more.

In our work we have seen that the "beyond-imaginable" things often come to us in little ways. The Bible in Zechariah 4:10 instructs us not to despise the day of small things, and God has repeatedly shown us that "you see the most of life through the smallest of windows."* He has reminded us that we cannot all do great things, but we can do small things with great love. Mostly, he has given us the special treasure of weakness, the packing of God's power, to accomplish his purposes.

And so, in the midst of a vast and complex city, I have found that it is the little things God has shown me that keep me going. I've learned from being here that whatever success we can claim

---

* F. Scott Fitzgerald

is not based on how spiritual we seem or how much we know the Bible or even how long we've been Christians. Our neighbors have told us more times than I can remember that if you want to see things change, stick around a good long while. It might just happen. I think any successes have occurred simply because God uses weak people who stick around for awhile.

As a result of "sticking around," we've learned a whole lot more from reading the Bible. We've learned about a fugitive with a shepherd's staff, a boy with five little stones, a widow with some pennies, a child with five hamburger buns and two sardines, and a woman looking for a lost coin. We have also learned by reading the human heart: about a frightened man with a butcher knife, a squatter with a mail-order ordination, an old man with nothing but his dogs and an old woman with everything but a dog, and a group of two or three kids in a hot storefront. We've learned how to be a church called Graffiti.

Hot dog, this is it!

Author's Note

All royalties from this book go to Graffiti Community Ministries, Inc., which is the service arm of the East Seventh Baptist Church nicknamed "Graffiti" on the Lower East Side of Manhattan. Graffiti continues to work to share the good news of Jesus Christ, provide emergency help for the homeless, offer education opportunities for children and youth, administer job development programs, and engage in Christian discipleship. If you wish to make a contribution to our ministry, you may make the check payable to:

Graffiti Community Ministries
184 E. Seventh Street, #2
New York, NY 10009

For more information, please call (212) 473-0044. Our Web address is: www.graffitichurch.org

Additional Resources

Abu-Lughod, Janet L., et.al. *From Urban Village to East Village: The Battle for New York's Lower East Side.* Cambridge: Blackwell, 1994.

Bakke, Raymond J. *A Theology as Big as the City.* Downer's Grove, Ill.: Intervarsity, Press, 1997.

———. *The Urban Christian.* Downer's Grove, Ill.: Intervarsity Press, 1987.

Christensen, Michael J. *City Streets, City People: A Call for Compassion.* Nashville: Abingdon, 1988.

Create a Safer World: Ideas for Reducing Violence in Your Community. Birmingham: Woman's Missionary Union, 1998.

Grigg, Viv. *Companion to the Poor.* Monrovia, California: MARS, 1990.

Linthecum, Robert C. *City of God, City of Satan: A Biblical Theology of the Urban Church.* Grand Rapids: Zondervan Publishing House, 1991.